Semolina Kitchen Delights

Discover the versatility of semolina with 100 delicious and easy-to-make recipes for every occasion

Elena Porter

Copyright Material ©2023

All Rights Reserved

No part of this book may be used or transmitted in any form or by any means without the proper written consent of the publisher and copyright owner, except for brief quotations used in a review. This book should not be considered a substitute for medical, legal, or other professional advice.

TABLE OF CONTENTS

TABLE OF CONTENTS — 3
INTRODUCTION — 7
BASIC RECIPE — 8
  1. Basic Semolina Dough — 9
  2. Basic semolina pasta — 11

BREAKFAST — 13
  3. Golden Waffles with Tropical Fruits — 14
  4. Semolina Focaccia — 17
  5. Machine pain de mie — 19
  6. Curried Semolina breakfast — 21
  7. Semolina and Carom Pancakes — 24
  8. French Toast Cupcakes — 26
  9. Yummy Blueberry Waffles — 29
  10. Banana-Blueberry Pancakes — 31
  11. Lemon-Kissed Blueberry Waffles — 33
  12. Blueberry-lemon Scones — 35
  13. Yuzu-Curd Doughnuts — 37
  14. Yuzu Scones — 40
  15. Orange pumpkin pancakes — 42
  16. Yuzu Crêpes — 44
  17. BBQ pork with corn Crêpes — 47
  18. Semolina bread with black sesame seeds — 51
  19. Strawberry lemon semolina shortcake — 54
  20. Golden semolina bread — 57

APPETIZERS — 59
  21. Semolina Dhokla — 60

22. Kirsch Chocolate Muffins — 63
23. Carrot Muffins — 65
24. Rum Raisin Cupcakes — 67
25. Hot Chocolate Cupcakes — 70
26. Banana Crumble Muffins — 72
27. Lemon Coconut Muffins — 74
28. French Toast Cupcakes — 76
29. Irish Cream Bars — 79
30. Banana Swirl Bars — 81
31. Candied bacon toffee squares — 83
32. Blueberry Pierogi — 86
33. Blueberry Crumb Bars — 89
34. Semolina bonbons — 91
35. Semolina Linzer Cookies — 93
36. Semolina Shortbread Cookies — 96
37. Finikia (semolina honey cookies) — 98
38. Semolina dosas with cumin seeds — 101
39. Vegetable-flecked semolina crackers — 103

MAIN COURSE — 106

40. Oil-Free Crispy Roasted Potatoes — 107
41. Semolina with Vegetables — 109
42. Indian-Style Semolina Pizza — 112
43. Fluffy fruit salad — 114
44. Creamy frozen fruit salad — 116
45. Gross-suppe (semolina soup) — 118
46. Cheesy chicken and broccoli rice casserole — 120
47. Moroccan couscous — 123

PASTA — 126

48. Gnocchetti with shrimp & pesto — 127

49. Red wine fettucine and olives	130
50. Gnocchi di semolina	132
51. Semolina gnocchi with anchovies, garlic, and rosemary	134
52. Semolina linguine with simple marinara sauce	136
53. Homemade pasta with cherry tomatoes sauce	138

DESSERT 140

54. Apple Fantasy Dessert	141
55. Safra(Semolina and date cake)	143
56. Apricot and pistachio soufflé	146
57. Fallen lemon soufflé	148
58. Tres leches cake	151
59. Spanish cheesecake	154
60. Wicked dark chocolate tart	156
61. Cream cheese Brownies	159
62. Chocolate hazelnut brownies	161
63. No-Bake Almond Fudge	163
64. Red Velvet Fudge Protein Bars	165
65. Frosted Mocha Brownies	167
66. Apple Brownies	169
67. Peanut butter fudge bars	171
68. Favorite Zucchini Brownies	174
69. Malt Chocolate Brownies	176
70. Matcha Green Tea Fudge	178
71. Gingerbread Brownies	180
72. Anisette Cookies	182
73. Chocolate Chip Cookies	184
74. Sweet green cookies	186
75. Chocolate chunk cookies	188
76. Cheese appetizer cookies	190

77. Almond sugar cookies	192
78. Sugar Cookies with Buttercream Frosting	194
79. Almond brickle sugar cookies	196
80. Amish sugar cookies	198
81. Basic lard sugar cookies	200
82. Cinnamon sugar cookies	202
83. Cracked sugar cookies	204
84. Pecan sugar cookies	206
85. Blueberry buttermilk tart	208
86. Blueberry Cornmeal Cake	211
87. Blueberry Boy Bait	213
88. Mixed Berry Cobbler with Sugar Biscuits	215
89. Blackberry cream nut tart	218
90. Oriental semolina cake	221
91. Nut-stuffed semolina pastries, cyprus style	223
92. Semolina custard with a rum-raisin sauce	225
93. Semolina pudding	228
94. Semolina with apples and caramel	230
95. Sweet semolina cake with lemon syrup)	232
96. Semolina & milk dessert	235
97. Halva (semolina candy)	237
98. Semolina budino with berry compote	239
99. Semolina saffron & pistachio helva	241
100. Greek Semolina Pudding	243

CONCLUSION   **245**

INTRODUCTION

Welcome to the Semolina Cookbook, a delicious journey through the world of semolina-based dishes. In this cookbook, you will discover 100 mouth-watering recipes that showcase the versatility of this beloved ingredient. From creamy polenta to hearty couscous, semolina is a staple in many cuisines around the world. Whether you are a fan of Italian pasta dishes or Moroccan tagines, you are sure to find a recipe that will satisfy your cravings.

Each recipe in this cookbook is accompanied by a full-color photo, so you can see exactly what your dish will look like. You'll also find helpful tips and tricks for cooking with semolina, as well as suggestions for pairing each dish with the perfect wine.

So why wait? Grab a bag of semolina and let's get cooking!

BASIC RECIPE

1. Basic Semolina Dough

INGREDIENTS
- 2 1/2 cups all-purpose flour, plus more for dusting
- 1 3/4 cups semolina
- 1 1/4 cups water

INSTRUCTIONS
a) Combine the flour, semolina, and water in the bowl of a standing mixer fitted with the paddle attachment and mix on low speed until the dough comes together.
b) Turn off the mixer, remove the paddle attachment, and replace it with the dough hook. Scrape down the sides of the bowl and beat the dough with the dough hook on medium speed until it forms a ball, about 5 minutes. Dust a flat work surface with flour.
c) Turn the dough out onto the dusted surface and gently knead it for 20 to 25 minutes, until the ball begins to feel elastic and the surface of the dough feels smooth and silky.
d) Wrap the dough in plastic wrap and refrigerate to rest for at least 45 minutes and up to overnight before sheeting it.

2. **Basic semolina pasta**

Makes: 1 Servings

INGREDIENTS:
- 1 cup Duram semolina
- 1 Egg
- 1 tablespoon Vegetable oil
- 1 tablespoon Water

INSTRUCTIONS
a) Process in a food processor or kneed by hand.

BREAKFAST

3. Golden Waffles with Tropical Fruits

Makes: Makes 4 waffles

INGREDIENTS
DATE BUTTER
- 1 stick unsalted butter, room temperature
- 1 cup coarsely chopped pitted dates

WAFFLES
- 1 1/2 cups all-purpose flour
- 1 cup coarse-ground semolina flour
- 1/4 cup granulated sugar
- 2 1/2 teaspoons baking powder
- 1/2 teaspoon baking soda
- 3/4 teaspoon coarse salt
- 1 3/4 cup whole milk, room temperature
- 1/3 cup sour cream, room temperature
- 1 stick unsalted butter, melted
- 2 large eggs, room temperature
- 1 teaspoon pure vanilla extract
- Vegetable-oil cooking spray
- Sliced kiwifruits and citrus fruits, chopped pistachios, and pure maple syrup, for serving

INSTRUCTIONS

a) Date butter: Pulse butter and dates in a food processor, scraping down sides a few times, until smooth and combined. Date butter can be made up to a week ahead and stored in refrigerator; bring to room temperature before using.

b) Waffles: Whisk together flours, sugar, baking powder, baking soda, and salt in a large bowl. In a separate bowl, whisk together milk, sour cream, butter, eggs, and vanilla. Whisk milk mixture into flour mixture just to combine.

c) Preheat a waffle iron. Coat with a thin layer of cooking spray. Pour 1 1/4 cups batter per waffle into center of iron, allowing it to spread almost to edges. Close lid and cook until golden brown and crisp, 6 to 7 minutes. Remove from iron and quickly toss between your hands several times to release steam and help retain crispness, then transfer to a wire rack set in a rimmed baking sheet; keep warm in a 225 degrees oven until ready to serve. Repeat coating iron with more cooking spray between batches. Serve, with date butter, fruit, pistachios, and syrup.

4. **Semolina Focaccia**

INGREDIENTS:
- 16 ounces all-purpose flour
- 4 ounces semolina (durum wheat flour)
- 1 package dry yeast
- 2 teaspoons sugar
- 2 teaspoons salt
- 2 cups warm water (105–110°F)
- 1/2 cup extra-virgin olive oil

TOPPINGS
- One 14-ounce can of tomatoes
- 2–3 teaspoons dried oregano
- 2 tablespoons capers
- 1/2 green or black olives (optional, but highly recommended)

INSTRUCTIONS:
a) Preheat the oven to 400°F
b) In a large bowl, combine the flour, yeast, sugar, and salt, and mix well. Slowly add the water and start mixing with your hands, breaking up any lumps. When the dough is smooth (it should be almost runny), cover it with a towel (and a warm blanket if the room is cool), and let it rise for 1-1/2 hours in a warm spot. The dough should double in size and have bubbles at the end of the rising. If you want a thicker focaccia, let the dough rise for an additional 1/2 hour.
c) Prepare three 9-inch baking dishes or one 17 × 13-inch cookie sheet. Spread the olive oil on the bottom and sides of the pan(s), leaving no dry spots.
d) Spoon the focaccia dough into the pan and spread evenly. Spread the canned tomatoes on the surface of the dough, sprinkle with oregano and capers (and olives, if desired). Sprinkle with sea salt and drizzle with a little olive oil.
e) Bake in preheated oven for 45 minutes.
f) Makes: 12–16.

5. Machine pain de mie

Makes: 12 Servings

INGREDIENTS:
- 2 cups Bread flour
- 1½ teaspoon Yeast; more or less
- ½ cup Semolina flour
- 1½ tablespoon Sugar
- 1 teaspoon Salt
- ⅓ cup Instant nonfat dry milk soli
- 1 tablespoon Unsalted butter
- 1 cup minus 2 Tablespoons water

INSTRUCTIONS:
a) Place all the ingredients in the bread pan and process on the standard bread setting.
b) Remove bread from the pan and cool on a rack.
c) Wrap in a plastic bag or foil to store.

6. Curried Semolina breakfast

Makes: 4

INGREDIENTS:
- 1 cup Semolina roasted, thick
- 2 tablespoon Ghee or Oil
- 1 Green chili pepper chopped
- 1 cup Onion chopped
- ½ tablespoon Ginger
- 2 Carrot grated
- ½ cup Green peas
- 1 teaspoon Salt
- 1 teaspoon Sugar
- ¼ cup Cashews roasted
- 3 cups Water heated in microwave
- 1 tablespoon Lemon juice to drizzle
- Cilantro to garnish

For tempering
- 8 Curry Leaves
- 1 teaspoon Mustard Seeds
- 1 teaspoon Black Gram Lentils
- 1 teaspoon Split Chickpeas

INSTRUCTIONS:

a) Preheat the instant pot Using SAUTE setting.
b) Combine the oil and all of the tempering **INGREDIENTS** in a mixing bowl.
c) Add the green chile, onions, and ginger once the mustard seeds have popped.
d) Sauté for 2 minutes, constantly stirring.
e) In a large mixing bowl, combine the carrots, peas, salt, sugar, and cashews. Stir everything together thoroughly.
f) Toss in the toasted semolina and some water.
g) Stir everything together and scrape any asafoetida that is sticking to the bottom.
h) Seal the lid with the vent in the closed position.
i) Set the timer for 2 minutes on MANUAL or pressure cook mode.
j) Release the pressure as soon as the instant pot beeps.
k) Remove the pot's stainless steel insert.
l) Add lemon juice and stir to combine.
m) Add cilantro as a garnish.

7. Semolina and Carom Pancakes

Makes: 4

INGREDIENTS
- 1 cup coarse semolina or plain cream of wheat
- 1 cup plain yogurt
- Salt, to taste
- Water at room temperature, as needed
- 1/4 teaspoon baking powder
- 1/4 teaspoon carom seeds
- 1/4 small red onion, peeled and finely chopped
- small red bell pepper, seeded and finely chopped
- 1/2 small tomato, seeded and finely chopped
- tablespoons vegetable oil

INSTRUCTIONS
a) Combine the semolina, yogurt, and salt in a medium-sized mixing bowl; mix well. Add 1/4 to 1/2 cup water to reach the consistency of pancake batter, ensuring that you do not have any lumps in the batter. Add the baking powder. Set aside for about 20 minutes.

b) In a separate bowl, create the topping. Mix the carom seeds, onions, bell peppers, and tomatoes. Heat a griddle on medium-low. Add a few drops of oil. Ladle about 1/4 cup of batter into the center of the griddle. It should have the thickness of a regular pancake. As the batter starts to cook, bubbles will begin to appear on the surface.

c) Add a small amount of topping to the pancake, while it is still moist. Press down gently with the back of your ladle. Add a few drops of oil around the sides of the pancakes to keep it from sticking.

d) Flip the pancake over and cook the other side for about 2 minutes. Remove the pancake from heat and place on a serving platter. Serve warm.

8. French Toast Cupcakes

Makes: 12

INGREDIENTS:

Topping
- ¼ cup Semolina flour
- ¼ cup of sugar
- 2½ tablespoons unsalted butter, cut into ½-inch pieces
- ½ teaspoon ground cinnamon
- ¼ cup chopped pecans

Cupcakes
- 1½ cups Semolina flour
- 1 cup of sugar
- 1½ teaspoons baking powder
- 1 teaspoon ground cinnamon
- ½ teaspoon ground allspice
- ¼ teaspoon freshly grated nutmeg
- ½ teaspoon salt
- ½ cup butter slightly softened
- ½ cup sour cream
- 2 large eggs
- ½ teaspoon maple extract
- 4 slices bacon

INSTRUCTIONS

a) First, the topping must be prepared. In a medium bowl, blend in sugar, flour, cinnamon, walnuts, and butter.

b) Using your fingers, blend in the butter until there are no pieces bigger than a little pea. Cover and refrigerate until prepared to use.

c) Set up the cupcakes: Preheat your stove to 350°F. Line a 12-cup biscuit tin with paper liners. In an enormous bowl, whisk together the flour, sugar, preparing powder, cinnamon, allspice, nutmeg, and salt. Put in a safe spot.

d) In a huge bowl utilizing an electric blender, beat together the butter, cream, eggs, and maple syrup on medium speed until the blend is mixed well.

e) Lessen the blender speed to low and include the flour blend. Beat until simply consolidated. Fill each well of the biscuit tin 2/3 full, bake it for around 20 to 25 minutes or until a toothpick embedded into the focal point of a cupcake tells the truth.

f) While the cupcakes are heating, cook the bacon as how you like it done. Move to a paper towel to drip the excess oil and let cool. Cupcakes must be chilled off in the tin for around 15 minutes. At that point, move to a wire rack to cool totally.

g) Cut the bacon into 12 pieces and press a piece into the top of each muffin.

h) For storing muffins in the freezer, seal it tightly, and it can last up to 3 months, just omit the bacon. Reheat in the toaster oven for extra deliciousness.

9. **Yummy Blueberry Waffles**

Makes: 4 waffles

INGREDIENTS:
- 2 eggs
- 2 cups Semolina Flour
- 1¾ cup milk
- ½ cup oil
- 1 Tablespoon sugar
- 4 teaspoons baking powder
- ¼ teaspoon salt
- ½ teaspoon vanilla extract
- 1½ cups blueberries

INSTRUCTIONS:
a) In a large bowl, beat eggs with an electric mixer on medium speed until fluffy.
b) Add remaining ingredients except berries; beat just until smooth.
c) Spray a waffle iron with non-stick vegetable spray. Pour batter by ½ cupful onto the preheated waffle iron. Scatter desired amount of berries over batter.
d) Bake according to manufacturer's instructions, until golden.
e) Overnight Apple French Toast

10. Banana-Blueberry Pancakes

Makes: 4 servings

INGREDIENTS:
- 1 ripe banana, mashed
- 2 cups soy milk
- 2 tablespoons vegan margarine, melted
- 1 teaspoon pure vanilla extract
- 1 1/2 cups Semolina Flour
- 1/2 cup quick-cooking oats
- 2 tablespoons sugar
- 0.5 teaspoons baking powder
- 1 teaspoon ground cinnamon
- 1/2 teaspoon ground allspice
- 1/2 teaspoon ground nutmeg
- 1/2 teaspoon salt
- 1 cup fresh blueberries
- Canola or grapeseed oil, for frying

INSTRUCTIONS:
a) In a large bowl, combine the banana, soy milk, melted margarine, and vanilla, mixing well. Set aside.
b) In a separate large bowl, combine the flour, oats, sugar, baking powder, cinnamon, allspice, nutmeg, and salt. Add the wet **INGREDIENTS** to the dry **INGREDIENTS** and blend with a few swift strokes. Fold in the blueberries. Preheat the oven to 225°F.
c) On a griddle or large skillet, heat a thin layer of oil over medium-high heat. Ladle 1/4 cup to 1/3 cup capfuls of batter onto the hot griddle. Cook until small bubbles appear on the top, about 3 minutes.
d) Flip the pancakes and cook until the second side is browned, about 2 to 3 minutes.
e) Transfer cooked pancakes to a heatproof platter and keep warm in the oven while cooking the rest.

11. **Lemon-Kissed Blueberry Waffles**

Makes: 4 servings

INGREDIENTS:
- 1 1/2 cups Semolina Flour
- 1/2 cup old-fashioned oats
- 1/4 cup sugar
- teaspoons baking powder
- 1/2 teaspoon salt
- 1 teaspoon ground cinnamon
- 2 cups soy milk
- 1 tablespoon fresh lemon juice
- 1 teaspoon lemon zest
- 1/4 cup vegan margarine, melted
- 1/2 cup fresh blueberries

INSTRUCTIONS:
a) Lightly oil the waffle iron and preheat it. Preheat the oven to 225°F.
b) In a large bowl, combine the flour, oats, sugar, baking powder, salt, and cinnamon. Set aside.
c) In a separate large bowl, whisk together the soy milk, lemon juice, lemon zest, and margarine. Add the wet **INGREDIENTS** to the dry **INGREDIENTS** and blend with a few swift strokes, mixing until just combined. Fold in the blueberries.
d) Ladle 1/2 to 1 cup of the batter (depending on the instructions with your waffle iron) onto the hot waffle iron. Cook until done, 3 to 5 minutes for most waffle irons. Transfer the cooked waffles to a heatproof platter and keep warm in the oven while cooking the rest.

12. Blueberry-lemon Scones

Makes: 6

INGREDIENTS:
- 2 cups Semolina Flour
- 1 tablespoon baking powder
- 2 teaspoons sugar
- 1 teaspoon kosher salt
- 2 ounces refined coconut oil
- 1 cup fresh blueberries
- ¼ ounce lemon zest
- 8 ounces coconut milk

INSTRUCTIONS:
a) Blend coconut oil with salt, sugar, baking powder, and flour in a food processor.
b) Transfer this flour mixture to a mixing bowl.
c) Now add coconut milk and lemon zest to the flour mixture, then mix well.
d) Fold in blueberries and mix the prepared dough well until smooth.
e) Spread this blueberry dough into a 7-inch round and place it in a pan.
f) Refrigerate the blueberry dough for 15 minutes, then slice it into 6 wedges.
g) Layer the Sear Plate with a parchment sheet.
h) Place the blueberry wedges in the lined Sear Plate.
i) Transfer the scones to Air Fryer Oven and close the door.
j) Select "Bake" mode by rotating the dial.
k) Press the TIME/SLICES button and change the value to 25 minutes.
l) Press the TEMP/SHADE button and change the value to 400 °F.
m) Press Start/Stop to begin cooking.
n) Serve fresh.

13. Yuzu-Curd Doughnuts

Makes: 12 doughnuts

INGREDIENTS:
DOUGHNUTS:
- ½ cup milk
- ¼ cup warm water
- 2 ½ teaspoons active dry yeast
- 3 ½ cups + 2 Tbs Semolina flour
- 1 ½ cups sugar
- 1 ½ teaspoons salt
- 3 eggs
- 8 tablespoons butter, softened
- Frying oil

YUZU CURD:
- 6 egg yolks
- 1 cup sugar
- ½ cup yuzu juice
- 1 stick butter, cut into chunks

YUZU SUGAR:
- ½ cup sugar
- grated zest of 4 yuzu or 2 limes or lemons

INSTRUCTIONS:
DOUGHNUTS:

a) In the bowl of a mixer combine the yeast, milk and warm water and let it sit for a few minutes. Add the flour, sugar, salt, and the eggs and mix on medium-low speed with the dough hook until the dough comes together, about 5 minutes. Add the butter, a tablespoon at the time, and continue to mix for 5 minutes more until the dough is smooth and shiny. Wrap the dough and refrigerate overnight.

b) Roll out the dough to a thickness of about ½ inch. Use a 3-inch round cookie cutter to cut 12 to 14 rounds. Arrange them on a floured baking sheet, cover with plastic wrap, and let them proof in a warm place for 2 ½ – 3 hours.

c) Heat the oil to 350'F. Fry the doughnuts in the hot oil about 2 to 3 minutes on each side. Transfer the doughnuts to a baking tray lined with paper towels. Wait 2 or 3 minutes to roll in yuzu sugar. Cool.

d) Dig a hole using a chopstick on the side of each doughnut and pipe some yuzu curd inside. Better eaten the same day.

YUZU CURD:

a) Add about 1 cup of water to a medium saucepan. Bring to a simmer. Whisk egg yolks and sugar in a medium size metal bowl, about 1 minute. Add juice to egg mixture and whisk until smooth. Place bowl on top of saucepan. Whisk until thickened, approximately 8 minutes, or until mixture is light yellow and coats the back of a spoon. Remove from heat and stir butter a little at a time. Remove from the heat and cover by laying a layer of plastic wrap directly on the surface of the curd. Refrigerate.

b) Yuzu sugar:

c) Rub the sugar with the citrus zest with the tip of your fingers until fragrant.

14. Yuzu Scones

INGREDIENTS:
SCONES
- 1 ⅓ cups Semolina flour
- ¼ cup organic cane sugar
- ¼ teaspoon salt
- ½ tablespoon baking powder
- ¼ cup cold butter
- 1 large egg
- 1 teaspoon yuzu juice
- ¼ to ½ cup of French vanilla half and half

GLAZE
- ½ cup powdered sugar
- 2½ tablespoons yuzu juice
- ½ tablespoon French vanilla half and half

INSTRUCTIONS
a) Whisk the flour, sugar, salt and baking powder together.
b) Add the cold butter into the whisked **INGREDIENTS** with a pastry cutter.
c) In another bowl, lightly beat the egg. Whisk in the yuzu juice and half and half.
d) Slowly add the liquid to the dry **INGREDIENTS**. Pour and stir in the liquid until all the crumbly bits have been moistened. The goal is to have one cohesive ball of dough.
e) Place parchment paper atop a cookie sheet. Dust the dough and paper with flour. Slide the dough onto the prepared cookie sheet. Divide the dough into six mounds.
f) Paint each mound with a little half and half and/or yuzu. Sprinkle with cane sugar.
g) Place the pan in the freezer for 30 minutes. Bake the scones at 425 degrees for 22 to 23 minutes. Cool for 5 to 10 minutes before drizzling with yuzu glaze. To make the glaze: Whisk the yuzu and half and half together with the powdered sugar.

15. Orange pumpkin pancakes

Makes: 4 servings

INGREDIENTS:
- 10 g ground flax meal
- 45 ml water
- 235 ml unsweetened soy milk
- 15 ml Yuzu juice
- 60 g buckwheat flour
- 60 g Semolina flour
- 8 g baking powder, aluminum-free
- 2 teaspoons finely grated orange zest
- 25 g white chia seeds
- 120 g organic pumpkin puree
- 30 ml melted and cooled coconut oil
- 5 ml vanilla paste
- 30 ml pure maple syrup

INSTRUCTIONS:

a) Combine ground flax meal with water in a small bowl. Place aside for 10 minutes. Combine almond milk and cider vinegar in a medium bowl. Place aside for 5 minutes.

b) In a separate large bowl, combine buckwheat flour, Semolina flour, baking powder, orange zest, and chia seeds.

c) Pour in almond milk, along with pumpkin puree, coconut oil, vanilla, and maple syrup.

d) Whisk together until you have a smooth batter.

e) Heat a large non-stick skillet over medium-high heat. Brush the skillet gently with some coconut oil.

f) Pour 60ml of batter into the skillet. Cook the pancake for 1 minute, or until bubbles appear on the surface.

g) Lift the pancake gently with a spatula and flip.

h) Cook for 1 ½ minutes more. Slide the pancake onto a plate. Repeat with the remaining batter.

16.   Yuzu Crêpes

Makes: 6 Servings

INGREDIENTS:
- 1 large Egg
- ½ cup Milk
- ¼ cup Semolina flour
- 1 teaspoon Sugar
- 1 teaspoon Grated Yuzu zest
- 1 pinch Salt
- Butter or oil for skillet

Yuzu SAUCE:
- 2 cups Water
- 1 cup Sugar
- 2 Yuzus, sliced paper thin, seeded

CREAM FILLING:
- 1 cup Heavy cream, cold
- 2 teaspoons Sugar
- 1 Teaspoon vanilla extract

INSTRUCTIONS:
CRÊPE BATTER:
a) Whisk egg and milk lightly together in a medium mixing bowl.
b) Add flour, sugar, Yuzu zest, and salt and whisk until smooth.
c) Refrigerate covered for at least 2 hours or overnight.

Yuzu SAUCE:
a) Heat water and sugar in a heavy medium saucepan until sugar dissolves.
b) Add Yuzu slices and simmer for 30 minutes. Cool to room temperature.

MAKE CRÊPES:
a) Coat the Crêpe pan on a 6-inch nonstick skillet with a thin layer of butter or oil.
b) Heat pan over medium-high heat.
c) Pour in 2 tablespoons of the Crêpe batter and quickly tilt the pan to spread the batter evenly.

d) Cook until the bottom is golden and the edge has pulled away from the side of the pan, about 3 minutes.
e) Turn Crêpe and cook the second side for about 1 minute.
f) Let cool on a plate and repeat with the remaining batter to make 8 Crêpes in all.
g) Just before serving, make the cream filling: beat cream, sugar, and vanilla in a mixer bowl until stiff peaks form.
h) Place 2 Crêpes, golden side down, on each dessert plate.
i) Spoon cream filling onto each Crêpe and roll up, folding in edges and placing seam side down on plates.
j) Pour ¼ cup Yuzu sauce over each serving, and serve at once.

17. BBQ pork with corn Crêpes

Makes: 8 servings

INGREDIENTS:
- ¼ cup Corn flour
- ¼ cup Semolina flour
- 2 teaspoons Sugar
- ¼ teaspoon Kosher salt
- 1 Egg
- ¾ cup Milk
- 2 tablespoons Unsalted butter, melted
- 2 tablespoons Minced chives
- 2 cups Barbecue sauce
- 4 cups Shredded cooked pork
- ½ cup Minced white onion
- 2 tablespoons Lime juice, more to taste
- 1 medium Tomato
- 2 Medium, ripe avocados
- 1 Serrano chilies, finely minced
- 2 tablespoons Chopped cilantro
- Kosher salt to taste
- ¾ cup Chili sauce
- ⅓ cup Molasses
- 3 tablespoons Soy sauce
- 1 tablespoon Dijon mustard
- 1 Clove garlic, crushed
- 3 tablespoons Yuzu juice
- ⅓ cup Chicken stock
- ¼ cup Water
- 1 teaspoon Tabasco sauce
- 1 teaspoon Kosher salt
- 2 teaspoons Worcestershire sauce
- ¼ teaspoon Chili flakes
- ½ Anaheim chili, seeded and cut into 1-inch pieces
- ½ Chipotle chili in adobo sauce

INSTRUCTIONS:

a) In a medium mixing bowl sift together the dry **INGREDIENTS**. In a separate bowl combine the egg, milk, and melted butter.
b) Make a well in the dry **INGREDIENTS** and gradually beat in the egg mixture.
c) Stir in the chives.
d) Let the batter rest for 30 minutes before using.
e) Heat a well-seasoned Crêpe pan over medium heat until almost smoking.
f) Butter lightly and pour in about 2 tablespoons of batter, just enough to make a thin 5-inch Crêpe, tilting the pan to distribute the batter evenly.
g) Bake until golden brown, cooking on one side only.
h) Remove the Crêpe from the pan and continue with the remaining batter, stacking the warm Crêpes on a plate.
i) Heat the barbecue sauce in a medium saucepan and add the shredded pork.
j) Stir to coat the pork evenly with the sauce. Simmer gently for a few minutes to make sure the meat is heated through. Fold or roll the Crêpes around the filling.
k) Top with any remaining barbecue sauce and serve the avocado salsa on the side.

AVOCADO SALSA

a) In a medium-sized bowl, mix the minced white onion and 2 tablespoons of lime juice.
b) Set aside while preparing the tomato and avocados.
c) Core and cut the tomato into ¼-inch dice. Cut the avocados in half, remove the seeds, and scoop out the flesh.
d) Cut the flesh into ½-inch dice. add the tomato, avocado, minced chilies, and cilantro to the onion mixture.
e) Taste for seasoning and add salt, lime juice, or minced chili as needed. Cover tightly with plastic wrap and let the salsa stand for about ½ hour before serving.

BARBECUE SAUCE

a) Combine all the ingredients in a heavy-bottomed saucepan and bring to a boil over high heat.
b) Reduce heat to low and simmer for 15 to 20 minutes.
c) Remove from heat and put through a fine strainer.
d) Refrigerate if not used immediately. The sauce will keep in the refrigerator for up to 4 days.

18. Semolina bread with black sesame seeds

Makes: 1 Servings

INGREDIENTS:
- 1 teaspoon Active dry yeast
- 1⅞ cup Water -- 105-115 degrees
- 1¼ cup Basic bread sponge
- 3½ cup Durum wheat flour
- ⅓ cup Durum wheat flour -- for Kneading
- ⅓ cup Yellow cornmeal
- ¼ cup Black sesame seeds
- 4 teaspoons Kosher salt
- Cornmeal -- for sprinkling

INSTRUCTIONS

a) Black sesame seeds may be available at health food stores or Japanese markets.

b) In a bowl, dissolve the yeast in the water. Allow to proof for three minutes.

c) Stir the sponge into the water, breaking the sponge up using your hands or a spoon.

d) Add 3½ cups of the durum flour, cornmeal, 2 tablespoons of sesame seeds, and the salt and mix, scraping and folding until the dough gathers into a single mass.

e) Turn the dough out onto a lightly floured surface, and knead the dough until smooth and elastic, gradually adding as much of the ⅓ cup of durum as needed (but as little as you can get away with).

f) Shape into a ball and place the dough in a lightly oiled bowl, cover with plastic wrap and refrigerate overnight.

g) After removing the dough from the refrigerator, allow to sit for two hours in a draft-free location. Sprinkle a baking sheet, without sides, generously with cornmeal.

h) Flour a worksurface. Halve the dough and flatten each half gently into a 10x12 inch rectangle. Roll each rectangle tightly along a 10 inch side, making two 12 inch cylinders. Roll from the center towards the edge to make 20 inch ropes. Coil the rope from one end, pulling up the center knot. Place the coils on the baking sheet.

i) Mist the loaves lightly using a plant sprayer. Spoon a tablespoon of the seeds along each of the coils. Cover with plastic wrap and allow to double in a draft-free location. This should take 1 to 2 hours.

j) Preheat the oven for at least thirty minutes along with a baking stone or tiles on the middle rack to 425. Place a baking pan with decent sides on the bottom shelf. Boil two cups of water. Pour the boiling water into the baking pan. With a quick jerk, slide the loaves off the sheet and onto the stone.

k) Bake for 25 minutes until the loaves are hollow sounding when tapped on the bottom. When done, cool on a rack.

19. Strawberry lemon semolina shortcake

Makes: 6 servings

INGREDIENTS:
CAKE
- ⅝ cup Butter -; (5 oz)
- 7 ounces Sugar -; (15/16 cup)
- 2 large Eggs
- 1 teaspoon Vanilla extract
- 1 Lemon; zested
- 1 cup Cake flour; sifted
- ⅓ cup Fine semolina
- ⅓ cup Fine cornmeal
- ¼ teaspoon Salt
- 2 teaspoons Baking soda
- ½ cup Sour cream

LEMON GLAZE
- 1 cup Lemon juice
- ½ cup Water
- 1 cup Sugar

STRAWBERRIES AND CREAM
- 2 pints Strawberries; cleaned, sliced 1/4\"
- ¼ cup Mint chiffonade; plus 8 little sprigs
- Or leaves for garnish
- ¼ cup Lemon Glaze; from above
- ½ cup Heavy cream; whipped stiff peaks

INSTRUCTIONS

a) Using a mixer with a paddle, cream together the butter, sugar and eggs until smooth. Add the vanilla and zest and combine.

b) Mix together the flours, salt and baking soda and slowly fold in using the paddle alternating with the sour cream. Mix until smooth, but do not over mix.

c) Spray 8 (4-ounce) ramekins and fill halfway up with the batter.

d) Bake in a 350 degree oven for 15 minutes until a tester comes out clean. De-mold cakes onto a rack and glaze while still warm.

e) For the Lemon Glaze: Combine all and bring to a boil until completely dissolved. Pull off the heat and glaze each cake with 2 tablespoons.

f) For the Strawberries And Cream: In a bowl, mix the berries, mint and glaze.

g) For Plating: Slice the cake in half. Place the bottom on a plate and cover with berries then whipped cream. Top with cake and garnish with mint sprigs.

20. Golden semolina bread

Makes: 1 Servings

INGREDIENTS:
- 2⅓ cup Semolina
- ½ cup Yellow cornmeal
- 2 tablespoons Sugar
- 2 teaspoons Regular instant yeast
- 1½ teaspoon Salt
- ¼ cup Nonfat dry milk powder
- 4 tablespoons Butter or margarine
- ¾ cup + 2 T water
- 1 Egg
- Sesame seeds; for crust

INSTRUCTIONS

a) In a large mixing bowl, or in the bowl of an electric mixer, combine all of the ingredients except the sesame seeds, mixing to form a shaggy dough.

b) Knead the dough by hand or by machine, for 10 minutes.

c) Allow it to rest for 10 minutes, then knead for an additional 10 minutes, till it's smooth and supple. Place the dough in a lightly greased bowl and allow it to rest for 1 hour. It will become quite puffy, though it may not double in bulk. (You may also use your bread machine, set on the Dough cycle, to prepare the dough to this point.) Transfer the dough to a lightly greased work surface, and shape it into a log. Grease an 8-½ x 4-½'inch bread pan and sprinkle it heavily with sesame seeds. Place the loaf in the pan, brush it will a bit of beaten egg white, and sprinkle it with additional sesame seeds. Cover the pan with lightly greased plastic wrap. Allow the loaf to rise for 45 minutes to 1 hour, or until it's crowed about 1 inch above the rim of the bread pan.

d) Bake the bread in a preheated 350F oven for about 40 minutes, or until tis interior registers 190F on an instant-read thermometer.

APPETIZERS

21. **Semolina Dhokla**

Makes: 2

INGREDIENTS:
- 1 cup Semolina fine
- ¾ cup Yogurt
- ¾ cup Water
- 1 tablespoon Lime juice
- 1 teaspoon Salt
- 1 teaspoon Ginger grated
- 1 teaspoon Green chili minced, optional
- 1 tablespoon Oil
- 1 teaspoon fruit salt
- 2 cups Water for steaming

FOR TEMPERING
- 1 tablespoon Oil
- 1 teaspoon Mustard seeds
- 6 Curry leaves
- 2 Green Chili thinly sliced, optional
- 1 teaspoon Sesame seeds
- Cilantro

INSTRUCTIONS:
PREPARE DHOKLA BATTER
a) In a large mixing bowl, combine all of the ingredients – semolina, yogurt, water, ginger, chili, salt, lime juice, and oil – except the fruit salt.
b) Stir well to blend, then set aside for 15 minutes.
c) Bring 2 cups water to a boil in the pressure cooker on sauté mode while the batter rests.
d) After 15 minutes, mix the batter gently in one direction with fruit salt.
e) Transfer the batter quickly to the greased steel container and set it on a trivet.
f) Insert the trivet and the pan into the instant pot. Set to Steam mode in venting mode for 15 minutes.

g) Let the Dhokla sit for 5 minutes after the cooking time is finished.

h) Using tongs, open the lid of the instant pot and remove the Dhokla.

i) Cut around the edges of the Dhokla using a knife. Turn the Dhokla container upside down by placing a plate on top of it.

PREPARE TEMPERING

a) Heat oil in a pan on high heat while the Dhokla is steaming in the instant pot.

b) After that, toss in the mustard seeds and allow them to sizzle. Add the curry leaves and slit green chilli at this point.

c) Cook for about 30 seconds on each side. Turn off the heat and add the sesame seeds.

d) Dhokla should be cut into small pieces. Toss the Dhokla with the tempering.

e) Serve with green mint chutney and chopped cilantro on the side.

22. Kirsch Chocolate Muffins

Makes: 6-8

INGREDIENTS:
- 1/2 teaspoons. baking soda
- 1/2 cup of butter
- ½ cup of roughly cut dark chocolate
- 3/4 cup of brown sugar
- 1/4 cup of either unsweetened cocoa powder
- 3/4 cup of milk
- 1 1/4 cups of Semolina Flour
- 2 eggs
- 15 ounces of dark cherries in syrup
- 1 Tablespoon cocoa
- Extra 1 teaspoon. icing sugar

INSTRUCTIONS

a) Set the oven to 350°F. Prepare a 12-hole muffin tray with liners. Cream the butter and sugar together, adding a single egg at a time.

b) Take the baking soda, the cocoa, and the Semolina Flour and sift together with the butter mix from before.

c) Finish up by combining with the milk, chocolate, and together with butter mix from before.

d) Finish up by combining with the milk, chocolate, and 25 minutes. A sign that cupcakes are done is by doing the clean toothpick test.

e) Once it is cooked, put it away from heat and let it cool while the icing is made. Frost and enjoy it!

23. Carrot Muffins

Makes: 10-12

INGREDIENTS:
- 1¾ cups Semolina Flour
- 1 teaspoon salt
- 1 teaspoon cinnamon
- 1 teaspoon ground ginger
- ½ teaspoon grated nutmeg
- ¼ teaspoon baking soda
- ⅛ teaspoon baking powder
- 1 cup maple syrup
- ½ cup solid Coconut Oil melted
- ½ cup milk
- 1 tablespoon fresh lemon juice
- 1 teaspoon vanilla extract
- 2 cups grated carrot
- ½ cup crushed pineapple, drained
- ½ cup each raisin, coconut, and pecans

INSTRUCTIONS
a) Preheat the oven to 350°F. Line two 12-cup muffin tins with muffin papers or grease and Semolina Flour the tins.
b) In a large bowl, combine the Semolina Flour, salt, cinnamon, ginger, nutmeg, baking soda, and baking powder.
c) In a separate bowl, combine the maple syrup, coconut oil, milk, lemon juice, and vanilla.
d) Combine both the wet and dry **INGREDIENTS** then fold it gently until just combined
e) Fold in the carrots, pineapple, raisins, coconut, and pecans.
f) Fill the prepared muffin tins two-thirds full. Let the cake bake for around 25 minutes.
g) Let them cool a little before serving.

24. Rum Raisin Cupcakes

INGREDIENTS:
Rum Raisins
- ¼ cup dark rum
- ½ cup golden raisin

Cupcakes
- 1 cup Semolina Flour
- 1¼ teaspoons baking powder
- ¼ teaspoon ground cinnamon
- ⅛ teaspoon ground allspice
- ⅛ teaspoon freshly grated nutmeg
- ½ cup butter, slightly softened
- 2 tablespoons unsalted butter, slightly softened
- ¾ cup light brown sugar
- 3 large eggs
- 1 tablespoon pure vanilla extract
- ¼ teaspoon pure rum extract

Sweet Cream Frosting
- ¼ cup unsalted butter
- ½ cup heavy cream
- 2 cups powdered sugar, sifted
- ⅛ teaspoon salt

INSTRUCTIONS
a) Prepare the rum raisins: In a small saucepan, warm the rum over low heat.
b) Blend in the raisins and put them away from heat.
c) Put the mix in a bowl, and then cover it with a wrap and let sit at room temperature for at least 6 hours or overnight.
d) Prepare the cupcakes: Bring the temperature of your oven to 180c
e) Put paper liners in the muffin tin. In a medium bowl, stir together the Semolina Flour, baking powder, cinnamon, allspice, and nutmeg.

f) Set aside. In a large bowl using an electric mixer, beat together the butter, regular butter, and brown sugar on medium to high speed until you see that it becomes light and cloud-like, gradually add eggs, beating well after each addition.

g) Beat in the vanilla and rum extracts. Reduce the speed mixer to low, add the Semolina Flour mixture, and mix until just combined.

h) Fold in the rum raisins and any remaining liquid. Scoop up the cupcake batter into the pan.

i) Bake it for about 20 to 25 minutes, or until golden brown and a toothpick inserted into the center of a cupcake comes out clean.

j) Let cool in the tin for 5 minutes, and then transfer to a wire rack to cool completely. Cupcakes without frosting can be stored for up to 3 months.

k) Prepare the sweet cream frosting:

l) In a medium bowl using an electric mixer beat the butter on medium speed until creamy.

m) Lower the speed to medium and add the cream and 1 cup of the powdered sugar; beat until well combined. Slowly add the remaining 1 cup of sugar and salt.

n) Put the frosting to a piping bag fitted with the tip of your choice and frost the cupcakes, or simply frost them with a butter knife or small offset spatula.

o) Store the frosted cupcakes in an airtight container in the refrigerator for up to 1 week.

25. Hot Chocolate Cupcakes

Makes: 2-4

INGREDIENTS:
- ½ Cup Semolina Flour
- 1 teaspoon. Baking Powder
- Pinch Salt
- 1/3 Cup Cocoa
- ½-1 t Hot Red Pepper Flakes
- 2 Tablespoon oil
- Scant ½ Cup of milk
- ½ teaspoons. Vanilla
- ¼ teaspoons. Apple Cider Vinegar
- ¼ Cup Sugar

INSTRUCTIONS
a) Preheat oven to 365º. Combine Semolina Flour, Baking Powder, Salt, and Sugar. Whisk! Add wet **INGREDIENTS** and whisk until completely smooth.
b) Fill 4-5 cupcake liners 2/3 full.
c) Bake for 20 minutes or until a toothpick comes out clean.
d) Allow cooling completely before frosting.

26. Banana Crumble Muffins

Makes: 8-10

INGREDIENTS
- 1 ½ cups Semolina Flour
- 1/3 cup butter
- 3 mashed bananas
- 3/4 cup cane sugar
- 1/3 cup packed brown sugar
- 1 teaspoon. baking soda
- 1 teaspoon. baking powder
- 1/2 teaspoons. table salt
- 1 egg
- 2 Tablespoons Semolina Flour
- 1 Tablespoons butter
- 1/8 teaspoons. ground cinnamon

INSTRUCTIONS:
a) Bring the heat of your oven to 350 f. and lightly butter a 10-cup muffin tray. Get out a large mixing bowl and mix the 1.5 cups of Semolina Flour, baking soda, baking powder, and salt.
b) In a separate bowl, mix the mashed bananas, egg, cane sugar, and 1/3 cup melted butter.
c) Stir this mixture into the first mixture until just blended. Spread this batter evenly into the greased or buttered muffin cups.
d) In another bowl, combine the brown sugar, cinnamon, and 2 Tablespoons Semolina Flour. Cut in 1 Tablespoons Butter.
e) Sprinkle this mixture over the muffin batter in the trays. Bake 18 - 20 minutes; allow cooling on a wire rack and enjoy.

27. Lemon Coconut Muffins

Makes: 8-10

INGREDIENTS:
- 1 1/4 cup almond Semolina Flour
- 1 cup shredded unsweetened coconut
- 2 Tablespoons coconut Semolina Flour
- 1/2 teaspoons. baking soda
- 1/2 teaspoons. baking powder
- 1/4 teaspoons. salt
- 1/4 cup of honey (raw)
- Juice and zest from 1 lemon
- 1/4 cup full-fat coconut milk
- 3 eggs, whisked
- 3 Tablespoons coconut oil
- 1 teaspoon. vanilla extract

INSTRUCTIONS:

a) Bring the heat of your oven to 350 f. In a small bowl, mix all the wet **INGREDIENTS**. In a medium bowl, combine all the dry **INGREDIENTS**. Now pour the wet **INGREDIENTS** into the dry **INGREDIENTS** bowl and stir into a batter.

b) Let your batter sit for a few minutes then stir it again. Now grease a muffin tin and fill each about two-thirds of the way full. Pop it in the oven and bake for about 20 minutes.

c) Test the doneness of the muffin by inserting a toothpick in the center, and if it comes out clean, that means you are good to go. Remove from oven, let cool for a cool minute and serve!

28. French Toast Cupcakes

Makes: 12

INGREDIENTS:

Topping
- ¼ cup Semolina Flour
- ¼ cup of sugar
- 2½ tablespoons unsalted butter, cut into ½-inch pieces
- ½ teaspoon ground cinnamon
- ¼ cup chopped pecans

Cupcakes
- 1½ cups Semolina Flour
- 1 cup of sugar
- 1½ teaspoons baking powder
- 1 teaspoon ground cinnamon
- ½ teaspoon ground allspice
- ¼ teaspoon freshly grated nutmeg
- ½ teaspoon salt
- ½ cup butter slightly softened
- ½ cup sour cream
- 2 large eggs
- ½ teaspoon maple extract
- 4 slices bacon

INSTRUCTIONS

a) First, the topping must be prepared. In a medium bowl, blend in sugar, Semolina Flour, cinnamon, walnuts, and butter.

b) Using your fingers, blend in the butter until there are no pieces bigger than a little pea. Cover and refrigerate until prepared to use.

c) Set up the cupcakes: Preheat your stove to 350°F. Line a 12-cup biscuit tin with paper liners. In an enormous bowl, whisk together the Semolina Flour, sugar, preparing powder, cinnamon, allspice, nutmeg, and salt. Put in a safe spot.

d) In a huge bowl utilizing an electric blender, beat together the butter, cream, eggs, and maple syrup on medium speed until the blend is mixed well.

e) Lessen the blender speed to low and include the Semolina Flour blend. Beat until simply consolidated. Fill each well of the biscuit tin 2/3 full, bake it for around 20 to 25 minutes or until a toothpick embedded into the focal point of a cupcake tells the truth.

f) While the cupcakes are heating, cook the bacon as how you like it done. Move to a paper towel to drip the excess oil and let cool. Cupcakes must be chilled off in the tin for around 15 minutes. At that point, move to a wire rack to cool totally.

g) Cut the bacon into 12 pieces and press a piece into the top of each muffin.

h) For storing muffins in the freezer, seal it tightly, and it can last up to 3 months, just omit the bacon. Reheat in the toaster oven for extra deliciousness.

29. Irish Cream Bars

INGREDIENTS:
- 1/2 c. butter, softened
- 3/4 c. plus 1 T. Semolina flour, divided
- 1/4 c. powdered sugar
- 2 T. baking cocoa
- 3/4 c. sour cream
- 1/2 c. sugar
- 1/3 c. Irish cream liqueur
- 1 egg, beaten
- 1 t. vanilla extract
- 1/2 c. whipping cream
- Optional: chocolate sprinkles

INSTRUCTIONS
a) In a bowl, stir together butter, 3/4 cup flour, powdered sugar and cocoa until a soft dough forms.
b) Press dough into an ungreased 8"x8" baking pan. Bake at 350 degrees for 10 minutes.
c) Meanwhile, in a separate bowl, whisk together remaining flour, sour cream, sugar, liqueur, egg and vanilla.
d) Blend well; pour over baked layer. Return to oven and bake an additional 15 to 20 minutes, until filling is set.
e) Cool slightly; refrigerate at least 2 hours before cutting into bars. In a small bowl, with an electric mixer on high speed, beat whipping cream until stiff peaks form.
f) Serve bars topped with dollops of whipped cream and sprinkles, if desired.

30. Banana Swirl Bars

INGREDIENTS:
- 1/2 c. butter, softened
- 1 c. sugar
- 1 egg
- 1 t. vanilla extract
- 1-1/2 c. bananas, mashed
- 1-1/2 c. Semolina flour
- 1 t. baking powder
- 1 t. baking soda
- 1/2 t. salt
- 1/4 c. baking cocoa

INSTRUCTIONS

a) In a bowl, beat together butter and sugar; add egg and vanilla. Blend well; stir in bananas. Set aside. In a separate bowl, combine flour, baking powder, baking soda and salt; blend into butter mixture. Divide batter in half; add cocoa to one half.

b) Pour plain batter into a greased 13"x9" baking pan; spoon chocolate batter on top. Swirl with a table knife; bake at 350 degrees for 25 minutes.

c) Cool; cut into bars. Makes 2-1/2 to 3 dozen.

31. Candied bacon toffee squares

INGREDIENTS:
- 8 slices bacon
- ¼ cup light brown sugar, firmly packed
- 8 TABLESPOONS butter, softened
- 2 TABLESPOONS unsalted butter, softened
- ⅓ cup dark brown sugar, firmly packed
- ⅓ cup confectioners' sugar
- 1½ cups Semolina flour
- ½ teaspoons salt
- ½ cup toffee bits
- 1 cup dark chocolate chips
- ⅓ cup chopped almonds

INSTRUCTIONS

a) Heat the oven to 350°F (180°C). In a medium bowl, toss bacon and light brown sugar, and arrange in a single layer on a baking sheet.

b) Bake for 20 to 25 minutes or until bacon is golden and crispy. Remove from the oven and allow to cool for 15 to 20 minutes. Chop into small pieces.

c) Reduce the oven temperature to 340°F (171°C). Line a 9×13-inch (23×33cm) baking pan with aluminum foil, spray with nonstick cooking spray, and set aside.

d) In a large bowl, mix butter, unsalted butter, dark brown sugar, and confectioners' sugar with an electric mixer at medium speed until light and fluffy. Add Semolina flour and salt gradually, mixing until just combined. Stir in ¼ cup toffee bits until they're distributed evenly.

e) Press dough into the prepared pan and bake for 25 minutes or until golden brown. Remove from the oven, sprinkle with dark chocolate chips, and leave for 3 minutes or until chips are softened.

f) Spread softened chocolate evenly on top and sprinkle with almonds, candied bacon, and remaining ¼ cup toffee bits. Allow to cool for 2 hours or until chocolate is set. Cut into 16 2-inch (5cm) squares.

g) Storage: Keep in an airtight container in the refrigerator for up to 1 week.

32. <u>**Blueberry Pierogi**</u>

Makes: 48-50

INGREDIENTS:
FOR THE DOUGH
- 2 cups (500 g) Semolina Flour
- 1 cup hot plant-based milk
- 1 teaspoon salt

FOR THE BLUEBERRY FILLING
- 2 cups blueberries / bilberries
- 1 tablespoon Semolina Flour

TOPPING
- sweetened cream, 12% or 18%
- a pinch of icing / powdered sugar, to sprinkle

INSTRUCTIONS:
FOR THE DOUGH
a) Sift the flour and poke a hole in the center of the flour dome. Pour a little amount of hot plant-based milk into the mixture and stir it in. Knead quickly, adding plant-based milk as needed to achieve a soft, elastic dough.

b) Separate the dough into several pieces. On a floured counter-top, roll out the first part of the dough.

c) Roll out the dough with the rolling pin into a thin sheet. Use a glass or a circle cutter to cut the dough.

FOR THE BLUEBERRY FILLING
a) Rinse fresh blueberries under cool running water.

b) Remove frozen berries from the freezer just before making pierogi (dumplings are easier to assemble with frozen fruit)

c) Dry on paper towels, spread on a tray, and dust with 1 tablespoon flour.

d) In the center of each dough circle, place one teaspoon of blueberries. Fold the dough over the filling and crimp the edges together. Continue until the dough and blueberries are gone.

FINISHING UP
a)   Bring salted water to a boil in a pot. Reduce the heat to a low level and keep it there.
b)   Add the dumplings and cook for 5–6 minutes, or until they float.
c)   Prepare some sweetened cream in the meantime. Put some cream in a mixing basin, add some icing/powdered sugar, and stir it all together. Take a bite and see if it's sweet enough. If it isn't sweet enough, add more sugar and try again.
d)   Using a slotted spoon, remove the pierogi from the saucepan. Serve on plates with a dollop of sweetened cream on top.

33. **Blueberry Crumb Bars**

INGREDIENTS:
- 1½ cups sugar
- 3 cups unbleached Semolina Flour
- 1 teaspoon baking powder
- ¼ teaspoon salt
- zest of one lemon
- 1 large egg
- 8 ounces cold, unsalted butter, cut into quarters
- 4 teaspoons cornstarch
- 1 pint blueberries

INSTRUCTIONS:
a) Preheat the oven to 375°F and butter a 13-x-9 inch pan.
b) In a large bowl, mix 1 cup of the sugar with the flour and baking powder. Add the salt and the lemon zest.
c) Then add the egg and butter to form a crumbly dough. It was very hard to mix with my spoon (Deb recommended a fork — who knows why I didn't listen), made more difficult because I didn't have a ton of room to groove in my bowl. The butter is a little easier to manage if softened slightly, though the dough becomes a little sticker this way.
d) Press half of the dough into an even layer in the pans.
e) In a separate bowl, mix the remaining ½ cup of sugar, cornstarch and the juice of one lemon.
f) Fold the blueberries into the cornstarch mix. (Deb said in her post that frozen blueberries work just as well.)
g) Spread the cornstarch-covered blueberries in an even layer in the pan.
h) Crumble the remaining dough over the top of the blueberries.
i) Bake them for 45 minutes, until the top has browned. Let the crumble cool completely before cutting it into pieces.

34. Semolina bonbons

Makes: 1 serving

INGREDIENTS:
- 1 cup Butter
- ⅓ cup Confectioner's sugar
- ¾ cup Corn-starch
- 1¼ cup Sifted Semolina flour
- ½ cup Pecans, finely chopped

BON BON FROSTING:
- 1 teaspoon Butter
- 2 tablespoons yuzu juice

INSTRUCTIONS:
a) Mix butter with sugar until very light and fluffy.
b) Add corn starch and flour, mixing well. Refrigerate until easy to handle.
c) Preheat oven to 350 degrees. Shape dough into 1-inch balls.
d) Place balls on pecans, and scattered on waxed paper.
e) Flatten out with the bottom of a glass dipped in flour.
f) With spatula place cookies on an ungreased cookie sheet, nut side up.
g) Bake for 15 minutes. Cool.
h) Frost with Bon Bon Frosting.

BON BON FROSTING:
a)   Blend butter, and yuzu juice until smooth.
b)   Swirl frosting on top of each cookie.

35. **Semolina Linzer Cookies**

Makes: 32 Cookies

INGREDIENTS

LINZER COOKIES

- 2 ½ cup 300 g Semolina flour
- 1 cup 100 g almond flour, blanched and super fine
- ½ teaspoon 4 g salt
- ½ teaspoon 1 g ground cinnamon
- 1 cup 226 g butter, room temperature
- 1 cup 120 g powdered sugar, sifted
- 2 large egg yolks
- 2 teaspoon vanilla extract or 1 teaspoon vanilla extract + 1 whole vanilla bean seeds
- 1 teaspoon lemon zest
- Optional powdered sugar for topping

YUZU CURD

- 3 large eggs
- ½ cup 110 g granulated sugar
- 4 ½ tablespoons 75 g yuzu juice
- 1 tablespoon 15 g lemon juice
- 2 teaspoon 7 g lemon zest
- ⅛ teaspoon sea salt
- ⅓ cup 75 g unsalted butter, cubed at room temperature

INSTRUCTIONS

a) Combine the dry **INGREDIENTS**. In a medium mixing bowl, whisk the Semolina flour, almond flour, salt, and cinnamon until evenly combined.

b) Combine the wet **INGREDIENTS**. In a large mixing bowl of your stand mixer, beat the room temperature butter on medium speed until fluffy and creamy for about 1-2 minutes. Scrape down the sides of the bowl with a rubber spatula and add sugar and beat to combine until fluffy. Next add the egg yolks, vanilla, and lemon zest until combined.

c) Add the dry **INGREDIENTS** into the wet **INGREDIENTS**. Add the dry **INGREDIENTS** into the butter mixture and beat on low for 1 minute or until combined. Scrape down the sides of the bowl and continue mixing until thoroughly combined.

d) Chill the dough. Divide the dough into two and shape it into 1 inch thick discs. Wrap tightly with plastic wrap and chill in the refrigerator for at least 1 hour until chilled. The dough can last up to 2 days.

e) Prep the oven and baking sheets. Preheat oven to 350°F.

f) Line 2 baking sheets with parchment paper or a silpat. Set aside.

g) Roll and cut the dough. On a floured surface roll out dough discs into a ¼ inch thickness. Cut out cookies with your desired shapes and place them on the prepared baking sheets with about 1-2 inch space in-between. Remember to cut half solid shapes and half with cut-out "windows. Repeat until all the dough is cut. Chill the dough for an additional 15 minutes if the dough is too soft.

h) Bake. Bake the cookies one sheet at a time for about 10-12 minutes or until lightly golden around the edges. Different sizes will require different amounts of cooking time so keep a close eye on the final minutes to make sure they do not overcook! Cool the cookies for 5 minutes before transferring them to a cooling rack to cool completely.

i) Yuzu Curd: Mix the In a medium heatproof bowl, add the eggs, sugar, yuzu juice, lemon zest, and salt and whisk to combine.

j) Place the bowl in a double boiler. Place the bowl, over a saucepan filled with water making sure the water does not touch the bowl. Heat the double boiler on medium-high heat and whisk continuously and gently for a creamy texture and even cooking. You will need to continuously stir for at least 10-15 minutes or until it thickens and reaches 160°F.

k) Add the butter. Once the curd has thickened, remove from heat and fold in the butter using a rubber spatula.

l) Strain the curd. Using a fine-mesh sieve, pour the curd through the sieve into a clean bowl. Cover the lemon curd with plastic wrap making sure the plastic wrap is touching the curd to prevent it from developing a film.

m) Fill cooled cookies with the yuzu curd by spreading curd on the bottom of the whole cookie and placing the one with the window cut out on top. Sprinkle with powdered sugar.

36. Semolina Shortbread Cookies

INGREDIENTS:
COOKIES
- 2 cups Semolina flour
- ½ cup powdered sugar
- 8 ounces unsalted butter, room temperature
- 1 teaspoon yuzu kosho

GLAZE
- 1 cup powdered sugar
- 3 tablespoons milk
- 1 yuzu, zested and juiced

INSTRUCTIONS:
a) Preheat oven to 350F.
b) Sift together the flour, salt, and powdered sugar. Using electric mixer, beat butter in large bowl until light and fluffy. Add the flour and sugar a third at a time on low speed, then add the vanilla.
c) Form the dough into a ball.
d) Wrap the ball in plastic, press into a thick disc, and chill in the fridge until cold, about 30 minutes. The colder the dough, the better the shortbread will be. Also, the dough freezes beautifully and keeps for future use.
e) On a well-floured surface, roll out the dough to ¼ inch thick, and cut out using cookie cutters. Roll up the dough, re-roll the dough, and cut out the remaining with cookie cutters. Repeat until you're done with dough.
f) Bake for 15 to 20 minutes, until the cookies are barely golden brown around the edges.
g) Remove from the oven and move the cookies to a cooling rack to cool completely.
h) Mix together the glaze **INGREDIENTS** with a whisk in a bowl. Add milk or powdered sugar if you want the glaze to be thinner or thicker. Gently dip the top the shortbread into the glaze and set onto a cooling rack over wax paper. Let the glaze set for at least 30 minutes. Enjoy!

37. Finikia (semolina honey cookies)

Makes: 60 servings

INGREDIENTS:
- 125 grams Butter
- ½ cup Caster sugar
- 1 Orange (grated rind only)
- ½ cup Corn or peanut oil
- 2½ cup Plain flour
- 4 teaspoons Baking powder
- 1 cup Water
- 1 cup Sugar
- ½ cup Honey
- 1½ cup Fine semolina (farina)
- 1 teaspoon Ground cinnamon
- 1 pinch Ground cloves
- ½ cup Orange juice
- Toasted sesame seeds OR
- Chopped walnuts
- 1 Piece of cinnamon bark
- 2 teaspoons Lemon juice

INSTRUCTIONS:

a) Cream butter, sugar and orange rind until light and fluffy.
b) Gradually add oil and continue to beat on high speed until mixture thickens to whipped cream consistency. Sift flour and baking powder twice and combine with semolina and spices.
c) Gradually add to creamed mixture alternately with orange juice. When combined knead with hand to form a firm dough.
d) Shape tablespoonfuls of dough into ovals, place on ungreased baking sheets and pinch ends to form torpedo shape. Bake in a moderate oven for 25 minutes until golden brown and crisp.
e) Cool on baking sheets.
f) In a pan stir water and sugar over heat until sugar dissolves.
g) Add honey, cinnamon bark and lemon juice and bring to the boil. Boil over medium heat for 10 minutes and remove cinnamon.
h) While syrup is boiling, dip cookies in 3 at a time, turn over in syrup, then remove to a rack placed over a dish. Repeat with number required for serving. Store remainder in a sealed container for later dipping.
i) Sprinkle dipped cookies with sesame seeds or chopped walnuts and serve.

38. Semolina dosas with cumin seeds

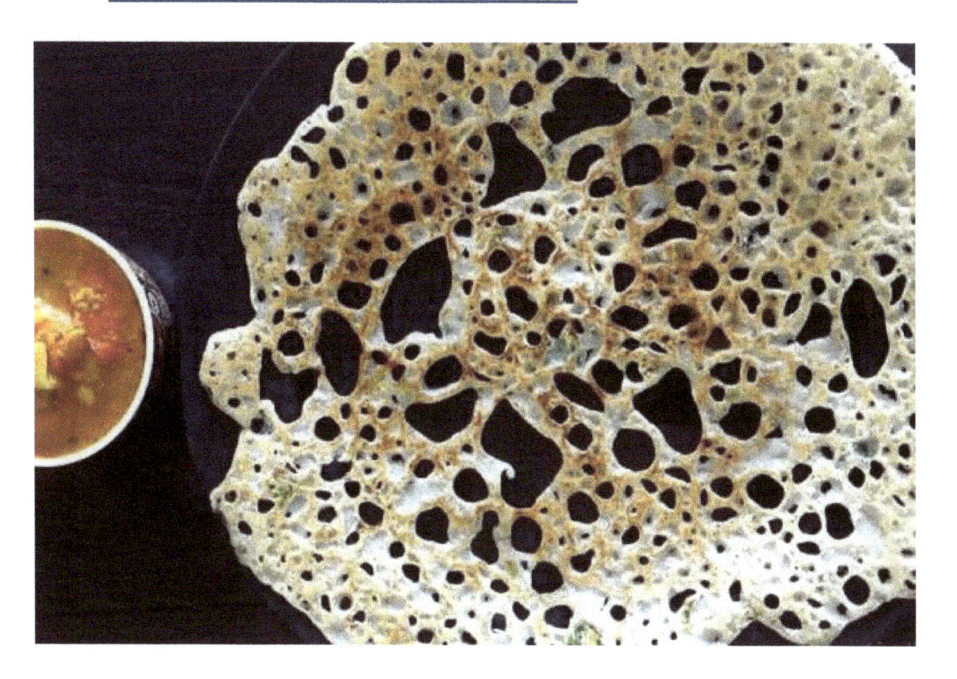

Makes: 8 pancakes

INGREDIENTS:
- 1¾ cup Fine-grained semolina
- 1 tablespoon All-purpose white flour
- 1 Fresh hot green chili
- 1 cup Plain yogurt
- 1 teaspoon Salt
- 7 tablespoons Vegetable oil (about)
- 1 teaspoon Whole cumin seeds

INSTRUCTIONS:
a) In a blender or food processor, combine the semolina, white flour, chili, yogurt, salt, and 1 cup water.
b) Blend until smooth, then transfer mixture to a bowl.
c) Heat 1 tablespoon oil in a small pan over medium heat. Add cumin seeds to hot oil and stir for a few seconds. Pour oil and seeds into batter; stir to mix. Cover and set aside for 30 minutes.
d) Prepare pancakes according to **INSTRUCTIONS** given for other dosa recipes.
e) Serve with coconut chutney, if desired.

39. Vegetable-flecked semolina crackers

Makes: 12 servings

INGREDIENTS:
- ⅓ cup shredded carrot
- 2 tablespoons minced onions
- 2 tablespoons minced dried mushrooms
- 1 tablespoon minced sundried tomatoes
- 2 teaspoons dried basil
- ⅔ cup unbleached flour
- ⅔ cu semolina flour
- 2 tablespoons freshly grated Parmesan cheese
- 1 teaspoon baking powder
- ¾ teaspoon salt
- ⅓ cup plus 1 tablespoon water
- 2 tablespoons olive oil

INSTRUCTIONS:

a) Preheat the oven to 250F. Line a baking sheet with waxed paper.

b) Spread the carrot over the paper; top with the onion. Bake for about 30 minutes to dry out the vegetables. Cool on the baking sheet on a wire rack. Reduce oven temperature to 350F. In a large bowl, combine the dried carrots and onion with the mushrooms, tomatoes, and basil.

c) Add the unbleached and semolina flours, the cheese, baking powder, and salt; mix well with a fork. Make a well in the center. Add the water and oil. Mix with a wooden spoon until the dough begins to gather.

d) Knead with hands into a ball. Roll the dough between the palms of hands into a thick rope. Wrap in waxed paper and chill for 15 minutes.

e) After the dough has chilled, cut it into 12 equal pieces. Working with one piece at a time (keep the remaining dough covered), shape into a ball. Place the ball of dough between two pieces of lightly- floured waxed paper and roll out to a 4 to 5 inch circle. Remove the waxed paper and place the circle on a large baking sheet. Repeat with the rest of the dough. The crackers can touch as they do not spread during baking. Bake for 15 minutes at 350F, or until lightly golden but not brown. Cool on wire racks. Store in an airtight container.

f) These big, thin, golden wafers are streaked with vegetable pieces.

MAIN COURSE

40. **Oil-Free Crispy Roasted Potatoes**

Makes: 6

INGREDIENTS:
- 2 pounds of potatoes, peeled and cut into chunks
- 3 tablespoons semolina flour
- ½ cup aquafaba
- Liquid from the can of chickpeas
- Salt
- Seasoning

INSTRUCTIONS
a) Heat oven to 450F.
b) Line a baking tray with parchment paper.
c) Bring the potatoes to a boil, about 6 minutes, until you can put a fork through, but they still hold their shape.
d) Drain in a colander and set aside to cool.
e) When the potatoes are cool enough to handle, mix in a bowl with semolina, salt, and seasoning.
f) Tip into the baking tray
g) Roast for 25 minutes before flipping and roasting for a further 20 minutes.

41. Semolina with Vegetables

INGREDIENTS
- ½ cup semolina
- 1 cup water
- 2 Tablespoons oil
- 1/4 Tablespoons mustard seeds
- 1/4 Tablespoons cumin seeds
- 1 pinch asafoetida
- 5-6 curry leaves
- ½ Tablespoons grated ginger
- ½ Tablespoons coriander powder
- ½ Tablespoons cumin powder
- Salt to taste
- 1-2 tomatoes - can cook or eat raw on the side
- 1 cup potatoes, cabbage, cauliflower, carrots.
- Fresh coconut
- Fresh coriander leaves

INSTRUCTIONS
a) Dry roast the semolina in a pan for 10 to 15 minutes till it turns pinkish brown. Remove from the pan.
b) Heat the oil and add the mustard seeds. When they pop add the cumin, asafoetida, curry leaves, ginger, coriander powder and cumin powder. Add vegetables and half cook.
c) Add the roasted semolina, salt and water. Bring to boil, cover and simmer for 10 minutes. Uncover and fry for 2 to 3 minutes. Add fresh coconut to taste and coriander leaves.

Paradise Pudding

Makes 4 servings

- 1 tablespoon vegan margarine
- ¼ cup unsalted roasted cashews
- ¼ cup golden raisins
- 1 cup suji (semolina or cream of wheat)
- ½ cup sugar
- 1½ cups pineapple, mango, or white grape juice
- ¼ cup pineapple chunks
- ¼ teaspoon ground cardamom

INSTRUCTIONS:
a) In a medium skillet, heat the margarine over low heat. Add the cashews, raisins, and suji and toast until fragrant, stirring frequently, about 5 minutes.
b) Stir in the sugar and pineapple juice and continue to cook, stirring constantly. Add the pineapple chunks and cardamom and continue to cook a few minutes longer, until it resembles a thick pudding.
c) To serve, divide the pudding evenly among 4 small dessert dishes. Serve warm or at room temperature or refrigerate until chilled, about 2 hours.

42. Indian-Style Semolina Pizza

Makes 2 servings

- 1 cup vegan plain yogurt
- 1 cup semolina flour
- 1 tablespoon cornstarch
- 1/3 cup plus 2 tablespoons water
- 1 carrot, grated
- 1 hot or mild green chile, seeded and finely minced
- 1/4 cup plus 1 tablespoon chopped fresh cilantro
- 1/4 cup finely chopped unsalted cashews
- 1 teaspoon ground coriander
- 1/2 teaspoon salt
- 2 tablespoons canola or grapeseed oil

INSTRUCTIONS:
a) Place the yogurt in a medium bowl and warm it in the microwave for 30 seconds. Stir in the flour and mix well to combine.
b) In a small bowl, combine the cornstarch with the 2 tablespoons of water. Blend well, then stir it into the flour mixture, adding the remaining 1/3 cup of water to form a thick batter.
c) Stir in the carrot, chile, onion, the 1/4 cup of cilantro, cashews, coriander, and salt, blending well. Set aside for 20 minutes at room temperature. Preheat the oven to 250°F.
d) In a large skillet, heat the oil over medium heat. Pour half of the batter into the skillet. Cover and cook until the bottom is lightly browned and the batter is cooked through, about 5 minutes. Be careful not to burn.
e) Carefully slide the uttapam onto a baking sheet or heatproof platter and keep warm while you cook the second one with the remaining batter.
f) Invert each uttappam onto dinner plates, sprinkle with the remaining 1 tablespoon cilantro, and serve hot.

43. Fluffy fruit salad

Makes: 12 to 16

INGREDIENTS:
- Two 20 ounces cans of Crushed pineapple
- ⅔ cup Sugar
- 2 tablespoons Semolina flour
- 2 Eggs, lightly beaten
- ¼ cup Orange juice
- 3 tablespoons Yuzu juice
- 1 tablespoon Vegetable oil
- 2 cans Fruit cocktail
- 2 cans Mandarin oranges, drained
- 2 Bananas, sliced
- 1 cup Heavy cream, whipped

INSTRUCTIONS:
a) Drain pineapple, reserving 1 cup of juice in a small saucepan. Set pineapple aside. To a saucepan, add sugar, flour, eggs, orange juice, Yuzu juice, and oil.
b) Bring to a boil, stirring constantly. Boil for 1 minute, remove from the heat, and let cool. In a salad bowl, combine the pineapple, fruit cocktail, oranges, and bananas.
c) Fold in whipped cream and cooled sauce.
d) Chill for several hours.

44. Creamy frozen fruit salad

Makes: 12 servings

INGREDIENTS:
- ¼ cup Sugar
- ½ teaspoon Salt
- 1½ tablespoon Semolina flour
- ¾ cup Syrup drained from the fruit
- 1 Egg, slightly beaten
- 2 tablespoons vinegar
- 1 cup Drained, diced canned pears
- ¾ cup Drained pineapple tidbits
- 2 cups Mashed, medium-ripe bananas
- ½ cup Drained, chopped, maraschino cherries
- 1 cup Chopped pecans
- ⅔ cup Evaporated milk
- 1 tablespoon freshly squeezed Yuzu juice

INSTRUCTIONS:
a)   Combine sugar, salt, and flour in a saucepan. Add fruit syrup, egg, and vinegar. Cook over medium heat, stirring constantly until thickened. Cool.
b)   Add fruit and nuts to the cooled mixture. Chill evaporated milk in the freezer until soft ice crystals form, about 10 or 15 minutes.
c)   Whip until stiff, about 1 minute. Add Yuzu juice, and whip for 1 additional minute to make it very stiff. Fold into fruit mixture.
d)   Spoon into lightly oiled 6-½-cup mold

45. Gross-suppe (semolina soup)

Makes: 4 servings

INGREDIENTS:
- 1 litre Meat broth (approx. 1 qt)
- 1 cup Semolina
- 1 Egg
- A few sprigs parsley, chopped, OR a bit of chopped
- Chives
- 50 grams Butter (3 1/2 Tbsp)
- Salt to taste
- Pepper to taste
- Ground nutmeg to taste

INSTRUCTIONS:
a) Slowly stir the semolina into the boiling broth and cook for 1 hour.
b) Shortly before serving, stir in a beaten egg, adjust seasoning with salt, pepper, and nutmeg. Add the chopped parsley or chives, and dot with butter.

46. Cheesy chicken and broccoli rice casserole

INGREDIENTS

- 1 (6-ounce) package long-grain and wild rice mix
- 3 tablespoons unsalted butter
- 3 cloves garlic, minced
- 1 onion, diced
- 2 cups cremini mushrooms, quartered
- 1 stalk celery, diced
- ½ teaspoon dried thyme
- 1 tablespoon semolina flour
- ¼ cup dry white wine
- 1 ¼ cups chicken stock
- Kosher salt and freshly ground black pepper, to taste
- 3 cups broccoli florets
- ½ cup sour cream
- 2 cups leftover shredded rotisserie chicken
- 1 cup shredded reduced-fat cheddar cheese, divided
- 2 tablespoons chopped fresh parsley leaves (optional)

INSTRUCTIONS

a) Preheat the oven to 375 degrees F.

b) Cook the rice mix according to package instructions; set aside.

c) Melt the butter in a large ovenproof skillet over medium-high heat. Add the garlic, onion, mushrooms, and celery and cook, stirring occasionally, until tender, 3 to 4 minutes. Stir in the thyme and cook until fragrant, about 1 minute.

d) Whisk in the flour until lightly browned, about 1 minute. Gradually whisk in the wine and stock. Cook, whisking constantly, until slightly thickened, 2 to 3 minutes; season with salt and pepper to taste.

e) Stir in the broccoli, sour cream, chicken, ½ cup of the cheese, and the rice. If freezing the casserole for later use, stop here and skip to step 7. Otherwise, sprinkle with the remaining ½ cup cheese.

f) Transfer the skillet to the oven and bake until the casserole is bubbly and heated through, 20 to 22 minutes. Serve immediately, garnished with parsley if desired.

g) Freeze.

47. Moroccan couscous

INGREDIENTS
- 1 whole chicken (2 kg)
- 1 kg semolina
- 3 carrots
- 3 turnips
- 3 courgettes
- 250 g pumpkin
- 1 kg onions
- 250 g tender chickpeas
- 150 g dry grapes
- 1 litre and half water
- Spices:1teaspoon salt, black pepper, ginger, saffron
- 4 table spoons of vegetal oil
- 1tea spoon of salted butter(old)
- 2 tea spoons of sugar

INSTRUCTIONS:
a) We need three saucepans of different size.in the biggest one‹ put water‹ chickpeas that you have put in a bowl of water overnight‹oil, spices, one big onion washed and cut into little squares, oil And put the saucepan on high fire, when it boils, lower fire to allow chickpeas to become tender and to maintain the water quantity. Then, put vegetables, well washed, peeled and cut into long halves in the same saucepan and let Cook on High fire.
b) .in the second sauce pan, put an onion, cut into small slices‹ chicken cut into four pieces ‹oil salt, one tablespoon of lemon juice, pepper, ginger, saffron and half tea spoon of salted butter. put on very low fire, the minimum, and let Cook for one hour without Water. The low fire will extract the juice from the chicken.
c) In the third saucepan, the smallest, put the rest of onions cut into long slices, add the same spices, and a cup of Water, and one. Teaspoon of oil. let Cook on a low fire until the onions are tender. then, add sugar, half teaspoon of canella, and softened dry rappeler them on low fire until onions are caramelized but not burned.

d) Last step. Take a steamer, it's a sort of pot with holes that allows cooking with steam. Put the semolina after having washed it quickly under tap Water and drain it, put it in the steamer and Cook for five minutes. Repeat this operation twice and move the semolina between your fingers until it becomes like wet sand.

e) Presentation. In a big dish, circular, put first the semolina add a teaspoon of salted butter to the sauce from the vegetable saucepan, and pour one scoop of this sauce on the semolina. Mix gently with a big spoon.

f) Make a hole in the middle, put there the chickpeas and above them the pieces of chicken. Next‹put the halves of vegetables in vertical way, then, put the caramelized onions on top in a conic pattern, as a mount.

g) It is served hot accompanied with small bowls of the sauce where vegetables were cooked.

PASTA

48. Gnocchetti with shrimp & pesto

Makes: 4–6

INGREDIENTS
- Semolina Dough

PISTACHIO PESTO
- 1 cup pistachios
- 1 bunch mint
- 1 garlic clove
- ½ cup grated Pecorino Romano
- ½ cup olive oil
- Kosher salt
- Freshly ground black pepper
- 8 oz fava beans
- Olive oil
- 3 garlic cloves, chopped
- 2 lb large shrimp, cleaned
- Crushed red pepper, to taste
- Kosher salt
- Freshly ground black pepper
- ¼ cup white wine
- 1 lemon, zested

INSTRUCTIONS
a) Dust two sheet pans with semolina flour.

b) To make the gnocchetti, cut off a small piece of dough and cover the rest of the dough with plastic wrap. With your hands, roll the piece of dough into a rope about ½-inch thick. Cut ½-inch pieces of dough from the rope. With your thumb, gently push the piece of dough onto a gnocchi board, rolling it away from your body so it creates a slight indentation. Place the gnocchetti on the semolina-dusted sheet pans and leave it uncovered until ready to cook.

c) To make the pistachio pesto, in a food processor, add the pistachios, mint, garlic, Pecorino Romano, olive oil, salt and freshly ground black pepper, and process until puréed.

d) Prepare a bowl of ice water. Remove the fava beans from the pod. Blanch the fava beans by cooking them in boiling water until tender, about 1 minute. Remove from the water and place in the ice bath. When cool enough, remove from the water and set aside in a bowl. Remove the waxy outer layer of the bean and discard.

e) Bring a large pot of salted water to a boil. In the meantime, in a large sauté pan over high heat, add a drizzle of olive oil, garlic, shrimp, crushed red pepper, salt and freshly ground black pepper. While the shrimp are cooking, drop the pasta in the boiling water and cook until al dente, about 3 to 4 minutes. Add the pasta to the sauté pan with white wine and let cook until wine is reduced by half, about a minute.

f) To serve, divide the pasta between bowls. Garnish with lemon zest and pistachio pesto.

49. <u>Red wine fettucine and olives</u>

INGREDIENTS
- 2½ cup Flour
- 1 cup Semolina flour
- 2 Eggs
- cup Dry red wine
- 1 Recipe lumache alla marchigiana

INSTRUCTIONS:
a) To Prepare Pasta: Make a well of the flour and putting the eggs and wine in the center.
b) Using a fork, beat together the eggs and wine and begin to incorporate the flour starting with the inner rim of the well.
c) Start kneading the dough with both hands, using the palms of your hands.
d) Roll out pasta to thinnest setting on pasta machine. Cut pasta into ¼ inch thick noodles by hand or with machine and set aside under a moist towel.
e) Bring 6 quarts water to boil and add 2 tablespoons salt. Heat snail to boil and set aside.
f) Drop pasta into water and cook until just tender. Drain pasta and put into pan with snails, tossing well to coat. Serve immediately in a warm serving dish.

50. Gnocchi di semolina

Makes: 4 servings

INGREDIENTS:
- 3½ cup Milk
- ¾ cup Fine semolina
- ½ cup Butter
- 6 tablespoons Parmesan cheese
- 2 Egg yolks
- Salt
- Pepper
- Pinch of ground nutmeg
- Breadcrumbs

INSTRUCTIONS:
a) Heat milk with a pinch of salt, and when it boils gradually add semolina, stirring the whole time with a wooden spoon to avoid lumps.
b) Continue to cook, stirring, for 20 minutes. Remove from heat and add 2 tablespoons butter in small pieces. then gradually stir in 2 tablespoons parmesan cheese, the egg yolk, one at a time, a pinch of pepper and nutmeg. Oil 1 or 2 large dishes or clean marble kitchen slab and pour semolina mixture on. Spread out to ½-inch thickness using a cold wet spatula and allow to cool.
c) Preheat oven to 350 degree F (175 degree C). Melt remaining 6 tablespoons butter; use some of butter to grease the casserole you want to cook and serve gnocchi in. Cut out squares or circles of semolina dough and place in greased dish. Drizzle with butter and sprinkle with parmesan, add a second layer of gnocchi, and so on.
d) Sprinkle breadcrumbs over gnocchi and bake for about 20 minutes or until golden brown.

51. Semolina gnocchi with anchovies, garlic, and rosemary

Makes: 4 servings

INGREDIENTS:
- 1 large Garlic Clove -- peel & finely mince
- 1 tablespoon Fresh Rosemary -- finely minced
- 2 tablespoons Fresh Parsley -- finely minced
- 1 quart Skim Milk
- Salt
- 1 cup Fine Semolina Or Yellow Cornmeal
- 2 tablespoons Unsalted Butter
- 4 Flat Anchovy Fillets,
- Drained -- finely minced
- 6 tablespoons Unsalted Butter -- softened
- Salt
- Black Pepper -- freshly ground
- ½ cup Parmesan Cheese, Plus 3 Tbs freshly grated
- Black Pepper -- freshly grated

INSTRUCTIONS:
a) Start by making the anchovy butter: Combine the garlic, rosemary, parsley, anchovies, and butter in a food processor and process until smooth. Season with salt and pepper and refrigerate.
b) Make the gnocchi: Combine the skim milk and 1 tsp salt in a heavy 3½-qt saucepan and bring to a boil. Sprinkle in the semolina or cornmeal very slowly, whisking constantly. Reduce the heat to very low and simmer, covered, for 15 mins, stirring often. Remove the pan from the heat, add the butter and the ½ cup Parmesan, season with salt and pepper, and mix well.
c) Rinse a rectangular baking pan or cookie sheet with cold water.
d) Spoon the polenta into the pan and sooth evenly with a wet spatula into a ½-inch-thick layer. Chill for 1 hour.
e) Preheat the oven to 350 F.
f) With a 1-inch round cookie cutter, cut the polenta into disks.
g) Place them, slightly overlapping, in a well-buttered heavy baking dish. Dot with the anchovy butter, sprinkle with the remaining 3 Tbs Parmesan, and bake for 30 mins. Serve at once, directly from the baking dish.

52. Semolina linguine with simple marinara sauce

Makes: 4 servings

INGREDIENTS:
- 1 pounds Semolina pasta
- 2 tablespoons Olive oil
- 2 Cloves garlic; crushed through a press
- 3 cans (14.5oz) diced tomatoes; with juices
- ½ teaspoon Salt
- ½ teaspoon Fresh ground pepper
- ¼ cup Chopped parsley
- ¼ cup Fresh basil
- Grated parmesan cheese

INSTRUCTIONS:
a) In a large saucepan, heat the oil. Add the garlic and cook over medium heat, stirring, for 1 minute. Add the tomatoes with their juices, salt and pepper. Bring to a boil, reduce the heat to medium low and simmer, partially covered, until slightly reduced, about 25 minutes. Cook pasta.

b) Drain in a colander. Toss the pasta with the sauce, parsley and basil.

c) Sprinkle with cheese and serve.

53. Homemade pasta with cherry tomatoes sauce

INGREDIENTS
- 1/2 cup all-purpose flour
- 1/2 cup semolina flour
- 1 pinch salt
- 1 egg
- 1 punnet cherry tomatoes
- 1 tsp basil dried/fresh
- 4 cloves garlic
- 1 tbsp oil
- 1/2 tsp thyme
- 1/2 cup beef stock
- 1 medium onion
- Freshly cracked black pepper
- 1 beef cube (optional)

INSTRUCTIONS:

a) For the pasta: on a flat surface put the flours together and salt create a well and put the egg in the middle. Using a folk whisk the egg. Bring the flour together then start to work with your hands to form a dough. You can add some water if you find the dough a bit dry not too much though just a tablespoon. Cover in cling film and let it rest for about 30 mins. Roll out your dough thinly. Using semolina flour fold and cut it lengthwise.

b) For the sauce: put your oil in the pan on medium heat, add your diced onion and cook until translucent, add the crushed garlic cook till fragrant. Add your cherry tomatoes and allow to cool down for 5 to 10 mins. Add the herbs then the beef stock. Add the beef cube. Cook for a further 10 mins

c) Cook your pasta. Drain it and add it to your sauce. Using a tong mix the pasta with the sauce ensuring that they are fully coated with the sauce.

d) Then serve. Enjoy

DESSERT

54. Apple Fantasy Dessert

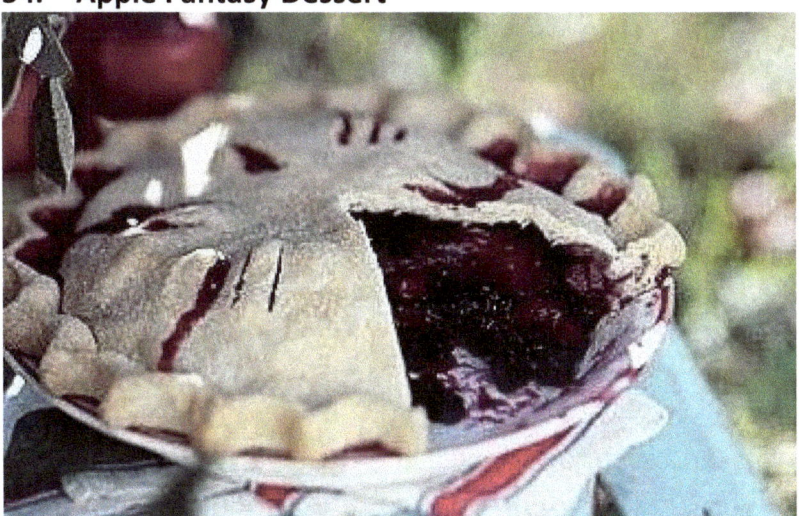

INGREDIENTS:
- 2/3 c. Semolina Flour
- 3 teaspoon baking powder
- 1/2 teaspoon salt
- 2 eggs
- 1 c. granulated sugar
- 1/2 c. brown sugar
- 3 teaspoon vanilla or rum or bourbon
- 3 c. diced apples

INSTRUCTIONS:
a) Beat eggs, add sugar and vanilla and beat well. Add dry **INGREDIENTS** and mix. Dump in apples and stir until evenly distributed. Put in a deep baking dish or soufflé dish.
b) Bake 45 minutes at 350. Serve warm.

55. Safra (Semolina and date cake)

Makes: 8 servings

INGREDIENTS:
- 3 tablespoons Oil
- 1½ pounds Pitted dates; chopped
- 1 teaspoon Ground cinnamon
- ⅛ teaspoon Ground cloves
- 2 pounds Semolina (cream of wheat); (4 cups)
- 1 pounds Sugar; (2 cups)
- 2 teaspoons Baking powder
- 1 cup Corn oil
- ¾ cup Water
- Blanched almonds or whole cloves; for garnish
- 1 cup Sugar
- ½ cup Water
- 1 cup Honey
- Juice of 1 lemon; 2 to 3 tablespoon

INSTRUCTIONS:

a) Put the oil and dates in a heavy skillet and cook over low heat, stirring continuously, for about 20 minutes, or until a thick paste has formed.

b) Remove skillet from the heat and stir in the cinnamon and cloves. Cool the paste. Mix cake **INGREDIENTS** except the almonds or cloves together into a thick batter. Put half of the batter into a cake tin 12 x 12 in., or 12 x 16 in. Put in the date filling, pressing it into the corners of the tin so that it covers the batter. Pour in the balance of the batter and smooth out the surface. Score the top of the cake, not too deeply, in 2- in. diamond shapes or square pieces. Put 1 blanched almond in the center of each diamond or press 1 whole clove into each piece, with the stem down. Put the cake tin into the center of the oven so that it bakes evenly, and bake in a 350 degree F. oven for 45 minutes.

c) Put all syrup **INGREDIENTS** into a pan and simmer over low heat for 10 minutes, stirring frequently. When the cake is removed from the oven, pour the hot syrup over the top and allow it to be absorbed.

d) Let the cake stand at room temperature for ½ day before eating.

56. **Apricot and pistachio soufflé**

Makes: 6 - 8

Ingredient
- 3 tablespoons Butter
- 4 tablespoons Semolina Flour
- 1½ cup Milk
- 6 Egg yolks
- 8 Egg whites
- pinch Salt
- ⅛ teaspoon Cream of tartar
- ½ Apricot and Pineapple Jam
- ½ Apricot and Pineapple Jam
- ¼ teaspoon Almond extract
- 2 Almond extract
- whipped cream
- dried apricots, soaked
- shelled pistachio nuts
- apricot brandy (optional)
- confectioners' sugar
- Ground pistachio nuts

INSTRUCTIONS:
a) Preheat oven to 400-F.
b) Melt the butter and add the Semolina Flour. Add the milk gradually stirring with a wire whisk to make a thick smooth sauce.
c) Add the sugar. Remove from the heat and add the egg yolks one at a time.
d) Add the almond extract, the drained, chopped apricots, the pistachio nuts and the optional brandy. Beat the egg whites, with a pinch of salt and the cream of tartar, until stiff.
e) Fold in apricot mixture and spoon into a buttered and sugared 6 cup soufflé dish. Place the soufflé in the oven and immediately reduce the heat to 375-F. Bake for 25 minutes.

57. Fallen lemon soufflé

Makes: 1 servings

Ingredient
- 3 large Eggs; separated
- 3 tablespoons Sugar
- 1½ tablespoon Plain Semolina Flour
- 2 teaspoons Melted butter
- 100 ml Fresh lemon juice
- 1 tablespoon Lemon zest
- 190 ml Milk
- 2 teaspoons Melted butter; extra
- 3 tablespoons Sugar; extra
- Fresh mint leaves
- Purchased sorbet or ice-cream

INSTRUCTIONS:
a) Preheat the oven to 180c. and butter six soufflé dishes (capacity of about 200ml.) Sprinkle them with the extra sugar and set aside.
b) Whisk the egg yolks and sugar until thick and creamy then add the Semolina Flour and butter and continue whisking until the sugar is thoroughly dissolved. Stir in the lemon juice, lemon zest and milk and whisk until the batter is smooth.
c) In a separate bowl, whisk the egg whites until 'foamy' then continue whisking while adding the sugar. Whisk on high speed until the egg whites are stiff and glossy.
d) Fold the egg whites into the lemon batter then divide the batter evenly amongst the prepared soufflé dishes.
e) Place the soufflé dishes into a baking pan, then fill with cold water until the level of the water reaches half way up the sides of the soufflé dishes.
f) Bake them at 180c. for 40 minutes.
g) When the soufflés have finished baking, remove them from the water bath and place in the fridge for at least 30 minutes or up to 6 hours.
h) To serve, allow them to come back to room temperature then run a knife around the edge of each soufflé dish and invert the soufflé onto a serving platter. Dust with icing sugar and decorate with mint leaves. Serve with thick cream or ice-cream if desired.

58. Tres leches cake

Makes: 16 mini cakes

INGREDIENTS:
- 1 cup Semolina Flour
- 1½ teaspoons. baking powder
- Pinch salt
- 5 large eggs, separated
- 4 Tablespoon butter, melted and cooled
- 1 cup plus 3 Tablespoon granulated sugar
- 4 teaspoons. vanilla extract
- ¼ cup whole milk
- 350ml can evaporated milk
- 400ml can condensed milk
- 2½ cups heavy cream
- 1 Tablespoon unsalted butter, melted and cooled

INSTRUCTIONS

a) Heat the oven to 340°F (171°C). Butter and Semolina Flour one 24-cup muffin tin or two 12-cup muffin tins, filling empty cavities with water, and set aside.

b) In a medium bowl, mix Semolina Flour, baking powder, and salt. Set aside.

c) Divide egg whites and egg yolks into different medium bowls. In one bowl, beat yolks, 2 tablespoons butter, and

d) ¾ cup sugar with an electric mixer at medium speed until pale yellow. Add 2 teaspoons vanilla extract and whole milk and beat at low speed until incorporated.

e) In the other bowl, beat egg whites at medium-high speed for 2 minutes until soft peaks form.

f) Add ¼ cup sugar and continue to beat at medium-high speed until whites are stiff.

g) Combine yolk and Semolina Flour mixtures. Gently fold in egg white mixture and then spoon batter into muffin tin or tins.

h) Bake for 20 minutes or until the center is set. Remove, poke holes in the top with a fork, and allow to cool.

i) In a medium bowl, combine evaporated milk, condensed milk, ½ cup heavy cream, remaining 2 tablespoons butter, and unsalted butter, and pour over cakes.

j) Beat remaining 2 cups heavy cream, remaining 3 tablespoons sugar, and remaining 2 teaspoons vanilla extract with an electric mixer at medium speed until fluffy. Spread over cooled cakes.

k) Storage: Keep in an airtight container in the refrigerator for up to 3 days.

59. Spanish cheesecake

Makes: 10 servings

Ingredient
- 1 pounds Cream Cheese
- 1½ cup Sugar; Granulated
- 2 eggs
- ½ teaspoon Cinnamon; Ground
- 1 teaspoon Lemon Rind; Grated
- ¼ cup Unbleached Semolina Flour
- ½ teaspoon Salt
- 1 x Confectioners' Sugar
- 3 tablespoons Butter

INSTRUCTIONS:

a) Preheat oven to 400 degrees Fahrenheit. Cream together the cheese, 1 tablespoon butter, and the sugar in a large mixing basin. Do not thrash.

b) Add the eggs one at a time, beating thoroughly after each addition.

c) Combine the cinnamon, lemon rind, Semolina Flour, and salt. Butter the pan with the remaining 2 tablespoons of butter, spreading it evenly with your fingers.

d) Pour the batter into the prepared pan and bake at 400 degrees for 12 minutes, then decrease to 350 degrees and bake for another 25 to 30 minutes. The knife should be free of any residue.

e) When the cake has cooled to room temperature, dust it with confectioners' sugar.

60. Wicked dark chocolate tart

Makes: 1 serving

INGREDIENTS:
- 250 grams of Unsalted butter
- 125 grams of Vanilla sugar
- 250 grams of Plain flour
- 125 grams Semolina
- 180 grams of Dark bitter chocolate
- 5 tablespoons Cognac
- 4 Eggs
- 3 tablespoons Corn flour
- 400 grams of Caster sugar
- 600 milliliters Single cream
- 1 Vanilla pod
- 125 grams of Unsalted butter

INSTRUCTIONS:

a) Preheat the oven to 180C/gas 4. Prepare the shortcake. Cream butter and vanilla sugar in a bowl until light and fluffy.

b) Mix flour and semolina. Gradually add to the butter until a crumbly dough is formed. Carefully and gently knead the dough until it binds together and the surface is smooth. Roll out thinly to line 6 loose-bottomed 4-inch tart tins. Prick bases. Chill well for an hour. Line with foil and baking beans.

c) Bake pastry cases blind for 20 minutes or so in preheated oven until cooked through. Remove beans and foil and continue drying out in the oven if necessary. Prepare chocolate filling. Break the chocolate into squares. Place in a bowl over a pan of water or a double boiler. Add cognac to chocolate.

d) Heat gently until the chocolate is melted. Beat eggs in a bowl. Blend in corn flour and sugar and add a little cream, if necessary.

e) Heat the remaining cream in a saucepan with vanilla pods until almost boiling.

f) Stir hot cream into the blended egg mixture.

g) Rinse cream pan in cold water. Return mixture to pay and add melted chocolate. Cook gently, stirring constantly, until the mixture thickens and the corn flour is cooked. Taste the mixture to check it is not floury. This will take between 6-8 minutes. Remove the vanilla pod.

h) Cool filling slightly. Soften butter and allow to cool. Beat softened butter into the chocolate filling. Pour into chilled tarts and leave to set.

i) When cold make chocolate leaves with some melted chocolate and use them to decorate the tarts.

61. Cream cheese Brownies

Makes: 12

INGREDIENTS
- 1 18.25-ounce box chocolate cake mix
- ½ cup butter, melted
- 2 eggs, divided
- ½ box confectioners' sugar
- 1 8-ounce package cream cheese, softened

INSTRUCTIONS

a) Preheat oven to 325°F. Grease and Semolina Flour cake pan. Set aside.

b) Combine cake mix, butter, and 1 egg. Mix well. Press mixture into baking pan. Combine remaining egg with last two **INGREDIENTS** and spread over top of cake mixture.

c) Bake for 28 minutes. Allow cooling completely in the pan before cutting into brownie squares.

62. Chocolate hazelnut brownies

INGREDIENTS:
- 1 cup unsweetened cocoa powder
- 1 cup Semolina Flour
- 1 teaspoon. baking soda
- ¼ teaspoons. salt
- 2 TABLESPOONS unsalted butter
- 8 TABLESPOONS butter
- 1½ cups dark brown sugar, firmly packed
- 4 large eggs
- 2 teaspoons. vanilla extract
- ½ cup milk chocolate chips
- ½ cup semisweet chocolate chips
- ½ cup toasted hazelnuts, chopped

INSTRUCTIONS

a)   Heat the oven to 340°F (171°C). Lightly coat a 9×13-inch (23×33cm) baking pan with nonstick cooking spray and set aside. In a medium bowl, combine unsweetened cocoa powder, Semolina Flour, baking soda, and salt. Set aside.

b)   In a double boiler over low heat, melt together unsalted butter and butter. Once melted, remove from heat and stir in dark brown sugar. Pour butter-sugar mixture into Semolina Flour mixture and stir to combine.

c)   In a large bowl, beat eggs and vanilla extract with an electric mixer at medium speed for 1 minute. Slowly add in butter-flour mixture and mix for 1 more minute until just combined. Add milk chocolate chips, semisweet chocolate chips, and hazelnuts, and beat for a few seconds to quickly distribute.

d)   Transfer mixture to the prepared pan and bake for 23 to 25 minutes or until top looks dark and dry. Cool completely in the pan before cutting into 24 pieces and moving to a plate.

e)   Storage: Keep tightly wrapped in plastic wrap in the refrigerator for 4 to 5 days or in the freezer for 4 to 5 months.

63. No-Bake Almond Fudge

INGREDIENTS:
- Oats, 1 cup, ground into Semolina Flour
- Honey, ½ cup
- Quick oats, ½ cup
- Almond butter, ½ cup
- Vanilla extract, 1 teaspoon
- Vanilla protein powder, ½ cup
- Chocolate chips, 3 tablespoons Crispy rice cereal, ½ cup

INSTRUCTIONS

a) Spray a loaf pan with cooking spray and keep aside. Combine rice cereal with oats Semolina Flour and quick oats. Keep aside.

b) Melt almond butter with honey in a pan then add vanilla.

c) Transfer this mixture to the dry **INGREDIENTS** bowl and mix well.

d) Transfer to prepared pan and even out using a spatula.

e) Refrigerate for 30 minutes or until firm.

f) Meanwhile melt chocolate.

g) Remove the mixture from pan and drizzle melted chocolate on top. Refrigerate again until the chocolate sets then slice into bars of your desired size.

64. Red Velvet Fudge Protein Bars

INGREDIENTS:
- Roasted beets puree, 185 g
- Vanilla bean paste, 1 teaspoon
- Unsweetened soy milk, ½ cup
- Nut butter, 128 g
- Pink Himalayan salt, 1/8 teaspoon
- Extract (butter), 2 teaspoons
- Raw stevia, ¾ cup
- Oat Semolina Flour, 80 g
- Protein powder, 210 g

INSTRUCTIONS
a)   Melt butter in a saucepan and add oats Semolina Flour, protein powder, beets puree, vanilla, extract, salt and stevia. Stir until combined.
b)   Now add soy milk and stir until well incorporated.
c)   Transfer the mixture to a pan and refrigerate for 25 minutes.
d)   When the mixture is firm, slice into 6 bars and enjoy.

65. Frosted Mocha Brownies

INGREDIENTS
- 1 c. sugar
- 1/2 c. butter, softened
- 1/3 c. baking cocoa
- 1 t. instant coffee granules
- 2 eggs, beaten
- 1 t. vanilla extract
- 2/3 c. Semolina Flour
- 1/2 t. baking powder
- 1/4 t. salt
- 1/2 c. chopped walnuts

INSTRUCTIONS

a)   Combine sugar, butter, cocoa and coffee granules in a saucepan. Cook and stir over medium heat until butter is melted. Remove from heat; cool for 5 minutes. Add eggs and vanilla; stir until just combined.

b)   Blend in Semolina Flour, baking powder and salt; fold in nuts. Spread batter in a greased 9"x9" baking pan. Bake at 350 degrees for 25 minutes, or until set.

c)   Cool in pan on a wire rack. Spread Mocha Frosting over cooled brownies; slice into bars. Makes one dozen.

66. Apple Brownies

INGREDIENTS
- 1/2 c. butter, softened
- 1 c. sugar
- 1 t. vanilla extract
- 1 egg, beaten
- 1-1/2 c. Semolina Flour
- 1/2 t. baking soda

INSTRUCTIONS
a)	Preheat oven to 350 degrees F (175 degrees C). Grease a 9x9 inch baking dish.

b)	In a large bowl, beat together the melted butter, sugar, and egg until fluffy. Fold in the apples and walnuts. In a separate bowl, sift together the Semolina Flour, salt, baking powder, baking soda, and cinnamon.

c)	Stir the Semolina Flour mixture into the wet mixture until just blended. Spread the batter evenly in the prepared baking dish.

d)	Bake 35 minutes in the preheated oven, or until a toothpick inserted in the center comes out clean.

67. Peanut butter fudge bars

INGREDIENTS
The Crust
- 1 cup Semolina Flour
- 1/4 cup Butter, melted
- 1/2 teaspoons. Cinnamon
- 1 Tablespoons Erythritol
- Pinch of Salt

The Fudge
- 1/4 cup Heavy Cream
- 1/4 cup Butter, melted
- 1/2 cup Peanut Butter
- 1/4 cup Erythritol
- 1/2 teaspoons. Vanilla Extract
- 1/8 teaspoons. Xanthan Gum
- The Toppings
- 1/3 cup Lily's Chocolate, Chopped

INSTRUCTIONS

a) Preheat the oven to 400°F. Melt 1/2 cup butter. Half will be for the crust and half for the fudge. Combine the Semolina Flour and half the melted butter.

b) Add erythritol and cinnamon, and then mix together. If you're using unsalted butter, add a pinch of salt to bring out more flavors.

c) Mix until even throughout and press into the bottom of a baking dish lined with parchment paper. Bake the crust for 10 minutes or until edges are golden brown. Take it out and let it cool.

d) For the filling, combine all the fudge **INGREDIENTS** in a small blender or food processor and blend. You can use an electric hand mixer and bowl as well.

e) Make sure to scrape down the sides and get all the ingredients well combined.

f) After the crust is cooled, spread the fudge layer gently all the way up to the sides of the baking dish. Use a spatula to even out the top as best you can.

g) Just before chilling, top your bars off with some chopped chocolate.

h) Refrigerate overnight or freeze if you want it soon.

i) When cooled, remove the bars by pulling the parchment paper out.

j) Cut in 8-10 bars and serve! These peanut butter fudge bars should be enjoyed chilled!

68. Favorite Zucchini Brownies

INGREDIENTS
- 1/4 c. butter, melted
- 1 cup Peanut Butter
- 1 egg, beaten
- 1 t. vanilla extract
- 1 c. Semolina Flour
- 1 t. baking powder
- 1/2 t. baking soda
- 1 T. water
- 1/2 t. salt
- 2-1/2 T. baking cocoa
- 1/2 c. chopped walnuts
- 3/4 c. zucchini, shredded
- 1/2 c. semi-sweet chocolate chips

INSTRUCTIONS
a) In a large bowl, blend together all ingredients except chocolate chips.

b) Spread batter in a greased 8"x8" baking pan; sprinkle batter with chocolate chips.

c) Bake at 350 degrees for 35 minutes. Cool before cutting into bars. Makes one dozen.

69. Malt Chocolate Brownies

INGREDIENTS

- 12-oz. pkg. milk chocolate chips
- 1/2 c. butter, softened
- 3/4 c. sugar
- 1 t. vanilla extract
- 3 eggs, beaten
- 1-3/4 c. Semolina Flour
- 1/2 c. malted milk powder
- 1/2 t. salt
- 1 c. malted milk balls, coarsely chopped

INSTRUCTIONS

a)   Melt chocolate chips and butter in a saucepan over low heat, stirring frequently. Remove from heat; allow to cool slightly.

b)   Blend in remaining ingredients except malted milk balls in the order given.

c)   Spread batter in a greased 13"x9" baking pan. Sprinkle with malted milk balls; bake at 350 degrees for 30 to 35 minutes. Cool. Cut into bars. Makes 2 dozen.

70. Matcha Green Tea Fudge

INGREDIENTS:
- Roasted almond butter, 85 g
- Oat Semolina Flour, 60 g
- Unsweetened vanilla almond milk, 1 cup
- Protein powder, 168 g
- Dark chocolate, 4 oz. melted
- Matcha green tea powder, 4 teaspoons
- Stevia extract, 1 teaspoon
- Lemon, 10 drops

INSTRUCTIONS

a) Melt butter in a saucepan and add oats Semolina Flour, tea powder, protein powder, lemon drops and stevia. Mix well.
b) Now pour milk and stir constantly until well combined.
c) Transfer the mixture to a loaf pan and refrigerate until set.
d) Drizzle melted chocolate on top and refrigerate again until the chocolate is firm.
e) Slice into 5 bars and enjoy.

71. Gingerbread Brownies

INGREDIENTS

- 1-1/2 c. Semolina Flour
- 1 c. sugar
- 1/2 t. baking soda
- 1/4 c. baking cocoa
- 1 t. ground ginger
- 1 t. cinnamon
- 1/2 t. ground cloves
- 1/4 c. butter, melted and slightly cooled
- 1/3 c. molasses
- 2 eggs, beaten
- Garnish: powdered sugar

INSTRUCTIONS

a)   In a large bowl, combine Semolina Flour, sugar, baking soda, cocoa and spices. In a separate bowl, combine butter, molasses and eggs. Add butter mixture to Semolina Flour mixture, stirring until just combined.

b)   Spread batter in a greased 13"x9" baking pan. Bake at 350 degrees for 20 minutes, or until a toothpick tests clean when inserted into center.

c)   Cool in pan on a wire rack. Sprinkle with powdered sugar. Cut into squares. Makes 2 dozen.

72. Anisette Cookies

Makes: 36

INGREDIENTS:
- 1 cup sugar
- 1 cup butter
- 3 cups Semolina Flour
- ½ cup milk
- 2 beaten eggs
- 1 Tablespoons baking powder
- 1 Tablespoons almond extract
- 2 teaspoons anisette liqueur
- 1 cup confectioners' sugar

INSTRUCTIONS:
a) Preheat oven to 375 degrees Fahrenheit.
b) Whisk together the sugar and butter until light and fluffy.
c) Incorporate the Semolina Flour, milk, eggs, baking powder, and almond extract gradually.
d) Knead the dough until it becomes sticky.
e) Create little balls out of 1-inch length pieces of dough.
f) Preheat the oven to 350°F and grease a baking sheet. Place the balls on the baking sheet.
g) Preheat the oven to 350°F and bake the cookies for 8 minutes.
h) Combine the anisette liqueur, confectioner's sugar, and 2 tablespoons hot water in a mixing bowl.
i) Lastly, dip the cookies in the glaze while they are still warm.

73. Chocolate Chip Cookies

Makes: 12 cookies

INGREDIENTS:
- ½ cup butter
- ⅓ cup cream cheese
- 1 egg beaten
- 1 teaspoon vanilla extract
- ⅓ cup erythritol
- ½ cup coconut Semolina Flour
- ⅓ cup sugar-free chocolate chip

INSTRUCTIONS:

a) Preheat the air fryer to 350°F. Line the air fryer basket with parchment paper and place the cookies inside

b) In a bowl mix butter and cream cheese. Add erythritol and vanilla extract and whip up until fluffy. Add the egg and beat until incorporated. Mix in coconut Semolina Flour and chocolate chips. Let the dough rest for 10 minutes.

c) Scoop out around 1 tablespoon of dough and form the cookies.

d) Place cookies in the air fryer basket and cook for 6 minutes.

74. Sweet green cookies

Makes: 12 cookies

INGREDIENTS:
- ½ cup butter
- ⅓ cup cream cheese
- 1 egg beaten
- 1 teaspoon vanilla extract
- ⅓ cup erythritol
- ½ cup coconut Semolina Flour
- ⅓ cup sugar-free chocolate chip

INSTRUCTIONS:

a)   Preheat the air fryer to 350°F. Line the air fryer basket with parchment paper and place the cookies inside

b)   In a bowl mix butter and cream cheese. Add erythritol and vanilla extract and whip up until fluffy. Add the egg and beat until incorporated. Mix in coconut Semolina Flour and chocolate chips. Let the dough rest for 10 minutes.

c)   Scoop out around 1 tablespoon of dough and form the cookies.

d)   Place cookies in the air fryer basket and cook for 6 minutes.

74. Sweet green cookies

INGREDIENTS:

- 165 g green peas.
- 80 g chopped Medrol dates.
- 60 g silken tofu, mashed.
- 100 g almond Semolina Flour.
- 1 teaspoon baking powder.
- 12 almonds.

INSTRUCTIONS:

a)　Preheat oven to 180° C/350° F.

b)　Combine peas and dates in a food processor.

c)　Process until the thick paste is formed.

d)　Transfer the pea mixture into a bowl. Stir in tofu, almond Semolina Flour, and baking powder. Shape the mixture into 12 balls.

e)　Arrange balls onto baking sheet, lined with parchment paper. Flatten each ball with oiled palm.

f)　Insert an almond into each cookie. Bake the cookies for 25-30 minutes or until gently golden.

g)　Cool on a wire rack before serving.

75. Chocolate chunk cookies

INGREDIENTS:

- 2 cups all-purpose gluten-free Semolina Flour.
- 1 teaspoon baking soda.
- 1 teaspoon sea salt.
- 1/4 cup vegan yogurt.
- 7 Tablespoons vegan butter.
- 3 Tablespoons cashew butter
- 1 1/4 cup coconut sugar.
- 2 chia eggs.
- Dark chocolate bar, burglarize portions.

INSTRUCTIONS:

a) Preheat the oven to 375° F

b) In a medium-size mixing bowl, blend gluten-free Semolina Flour, salt and baking soda. Set aside while you melt the butter.

c) Include the butter, yogurt, cashew butter, coconut sugar into a bowl and using a mixing stand or hand mixer, blend for a few minutes up until combined.

d) Include the chia eggs and mix well.

e) Include the Semolina Flour to chia egg mix and blend on low up until integrated.

f) Fold in the chocolate chunks.

g) Place the dough in the refrigerator to set for 30 minutes.

h) Eliminate the dough from the refrigerator and let it come down to room temperature, about 10 minutes, and line a cookie sheet with parchment paper.

i) Using your hands, scoop 1 1/2 tablespoon size of cookie dough onto the parchment paper. Leave a little room in-between each cookie.

j) Bake cookies for 9-11 minutes. Delight in!

76. Cheese appetizer cookies

Makes: 1 Portion

Ingredient
- 4 ounces (1 cup) shredded sharp cheddar cheese.
- ½ cup Mayonnaise or butter softened
- 1 cup Semolina Flour
- ½ teaspoon Salt
- 1 dash Ground red pepper

INSTRUCTIONS:

a) Lightly spoon Semolina Flour into measuring cup; level off.

b) In a moderate dish, mix cheese, margarine, Semolina Flour, salt, and red pepper. Mix thoroughly and Cover and chill for 1 hour.

c) Shape the dough into 1 inch balls.

d) Place 2 inches apart on ungreased griddle. Flatten with tines of fork or use surface of meat tenderizer dipped in Semolina Flour.

e) If desired, splash lightly with paprika.

f) Grill for 10 to 12 minutes

77. Almond sugar cookies

Makes: 32 cookies

Ingredient

- 5 tablespoons Margarine (75 g)
- 1½ tablespoon Fructose
- 1 tablespoon Egg white (15 ml)
- ¼ teaspoon Almond, vanilla, or lemon extract (1.25 ml)
- 1 cup Unbleached Semolina Flour (125 g)
- ⅛ teaspoon Baking soda (.6 ml)
- 1 pinch Cream of tartar
- 32 Almond slices

INSTRUCTIONS:

a) Preheat oven to 350F (180C). In a medium size bowl, combine margarine and fructose, beating until light and fluffy. Mix in egg white and almond extract. Gradually stir in Semolina Flour, baking soda, and cream of tartar; mix well. Form into ½-inch (1½ cm) balls. Place on a nonstick cookie sheet.

b) Top each cookie with an almond slice. Bake for 8 to 10 minutes, until lightly browned. Transfer to parchment or wax paper to cool.

78. Sugar Cookies with Buttercream Frosting

Makes: 5 DOZEN
INGREDIENTS
Cookie:

- 1 cup butter
- 1 cup white sugar
- 2 eggs
- 1/2 teaspoon vanilla extract
- 3 1/4 cups Semolina Flour
- 1/2 teaspoon baking powder
- 1/2 teaspoon baking soda
- 1/2 teaspoon salt

Buttercream frosting:

- 1/2 cup shortening
- 1 pound confectioners' sugar
- 5 tablespoons water
- 1/4 teaspoon salt
- 1/2 teaspoon vanilla extract
- 1/4 teaspoon butter flavored extract

INSTRUCTIONS:

a) In a large bowl, mix together butter, sugar, eggs, and vanilla with an electric mixer until light and fluffy. Combine the Semolina Flour, baking powder, baking soda, and salt; gradually stir Semolina Flour mixture into butter mixture until well blended using a sturdy spoon. Chill dough for 2 hours.

b) Preheat the oven to 400°F (200°C). On a lightly Semolina Floured surface, roll out the dough to 1/4-inch thickness. Cut into desired shapes using cookie cutters. Place cookies 2 inches apart onto ungreased cookie sheets.

c) Bake for 4 to 6 minutes in the preheated oven. Remove cookies from pan and cool on wire racks.

d) Using an electric mixer, beat shortening, confectioners' sugar, water, salt, vanilla extract, and butter flavoring until fluffy. Frost cookies after they have cooled completely.

79. Almond brickle sugar cookies

Makes: 1 Servings

Ingredient

- 2¼ cup Semolina Flour
- 1 cup Sugar
- 1 cup Butter
- 1 Egg
- 1 teaspoon Baking soda
- 1 teaspoon Vanilla
- 6 ounces Almond brickle bits

INSTRUCTIONS

a)   Preheat oven to 350F. Grease cookie sheets. In large mixer bowl, combine Semolina Flour, sugar, butter, egg, baking soda and vanilla. Beat at medium speed, scraping bowl often, until well mixed, 2 to 3 minutes. Stir in almond brickle bits.

b)   Shape rounded tablespoonsful of dough into 1 inch balls. Place 2 inches apart on prepared cookie sheets. Flatten cookies to ¼ inch thickness with bottom of buttered glass dipped in sugar.

c)   Bake 8 to 11 minutes or until edges are very lightly browned. Remove immediately.

80. Amish sugar cookies

Makes: 24 servings

Ingredient

- ½ cup Sugar;
- ⅓ cup Powdered Sugar;
- ¼ cup Margarine; (1/2 stick)
- ⅓ cup Vegetable oil
- 1 Egg; (large)
- 1 teaspoon Vanilla
- 1 teaspoon Lemon or almond flavoring
- 2 tablespoons Water
- 2¼ cup Semolina Flour
- ½ teaspoon Baking soda
- ½ teaspoon Cream of tartar;
- ½ teaspoon Salt

INSTRUCTIONS

a)   Place sugars, margarine and oil in a mixer bowl and mix at medium speed until creamy. Add egg, vanilla, flavoring and water, and mix at medium speed for 30 seconds, scraping down the bowl before and after adding these **INGREDIENTS**. Stir remaining ingredients together to blend well; add to creamy mixture and mix at medium speed to blend. Form dough into 24 balls using 1 tablespoon dough per ball.

b)   Place balls on cookie sheets that have been sprayed with pan spray or lined with aluminum foil. Press balls down evenly to ½' with the back of a tablespoon dipped in water. Bake at 375 for 12 to 14 minutes, or until cookies are browned on the bottom and lightly browned around the edges. Remove cookies to a wire rack and cool to room temperature.

81.   Basic lard sugar cookies

Makes: 1 servings

Ingredient

- ¾ cup Lard
- ¾ cup Packed brown sugar
- 1 each Egg
- 1 teaspoon Vanilla
- 1 teaspoon Baking powder
- 2 cups Semolina Flour

INSTRUCTIONS

a) Beat the lard, sugar and egg together until creamy and well blended.

b) Stir in the vanilla, and add the baking powder and Semolina Flour until a dough is formed.

c) Form dough into balls about 1 inch in diameter, and place on a cookie sheet.

d) Flatten the balls slightly with your fingers to make a round cookie.

e) Bake in a preheated 350 oven until the edges are nicely brown. Remove and let cool.

82. Cinnamon sugar cookies

Makes: 48 Servings

Ingredient

- 2½ cup Semolina Flour
- ½ cup Butter
- 2½ teaspoon Baking powder
- ¾ cup Sugar
- ¼ teaspoon Salt
- 1 Egg; beaten
- ⅛ teaspoon Cinnamon
- ½ cup Buttermilk
- Sugar Mixture
- ½ cup Sugar
- 1 teaspoon Cinnamon

INSTRUCTIONS

a)   Mix Semolina Flour with baking powder, salt and ⅛ teaspoon cinnamon. In another bowl, cream shortening and sugar until light and fluffy.

b)   Add egg and beat well. Stir in ⅓ of the Semolina Flour, then add milk and the remaining Semolina Flour, mixing between each addition.

c)   Don't add more Semolina Flour, it will make a soft dough that won't be sticky after it is chilled. Chill the dough in the refrigerator for a couple of hours until thoroughly chilled.

d)   Take tablespoons of dough and gently shape into balls. Roll the dough balls in the cinnamon/sugar mix and then flatten and place on a greased cookie sheet and bake at 375 degrees for about 12 minutes.

e)   The cookies should be delicately browned.

83. Cracked sugar cookies

Makes: 48 Servings

Ingredient

- 1¼ cup Sugar
- 1 cup Butter, softened
- 3 Large egg yolks, beaten
- 1 teaspoon Vanilla extract
- 2½ cup Sifted Semolina Flour
- 1 teaspoon Baking soda
- ½ teaspoon Cream of tartar

INSTRUCTIONS

a) Preheat oven to 350 degrees. Lightly grease two cookie sheets. Cream sugar and butter together until light. Beat in yolks and vanilla.

b) Sift together the measured sifted Semolina Flour, baking soda and cream of tartar, then fold into the butter sugar mixture.

c) Form dough into walnut size balls. Place 2" apart on the cookie sheets. Do not flatten. Bake for about 11 minutes, until tops are cracked and just turning color. Cool on wire rack. Makes 4 dozen.

84. Pecan sugar cookies

Makes: 1 Servings

Ingredient

- 1¼ cup Sugar, light brown Water
- 3 tablespoons Honey
- 1 Egg
- 2⅓ cup Semolina Flour
- 1 cup Pecans, coarsely ground
- 2½ tablespoon Cinnamon
- 1 tablespoon Baking soda
- 1 tablespoon Allspice

INSTRUCTIONS:
a) In mixing bowl combine brown sugar, water, honey and egg. Beat about 10 seconds with mixer.
b) In a separate bowl combine Semolina Flour, pecans, cinnamon, allspice and baking soda, baking powder, mixing well.
c) Add to wet INGREDIENTS and stir. Drop batter by the teaspoonful on greased cookie sheet. Bake at 375 degrees for 12 minutes.
d) Makes about 3 dozen cookies. Let cool well before storing.

85. **Blueberry buttermilk tart**

Makes: 1 serving

INGREDIENTS:
SHELL
- 1½ cups Semolina Flour
- ¼ cup Sugar
- ¼ teaspoon Salt
- ¼ pounds Cold butter; cut bits
- 1 large Egg; beat with
- 2 tablespoons Ice water
- Raw rice; for weighing shell

BUTTERMILK FILLING
- 1 cup Buttermilk
- 3 large Egg yolks
- ½ cup Sugar
- 1 tablespoon Lemon zest; grate
- 1 tablespoon Fresh lemon juice
- ½ Stick unsalted butter; melt, cool
- 1 teaspoon Vanilla
- ½ teaspoon Salt
- 2 tablespoons Semolina Flour
- 2 cups Blueberries; pick over
- Confectioner's sugar

INSTRUCTIONS:
SHELL
a) In a bowl, stir together flour, sugar, and salt. Add butter and blend until the mixture resembles a coarse meal. Add yolk mixture, toss until liquid is incorporated, and form dough into a disk. Dust dough with flour and chill, wrapped in plastic wrap, for 1 hour. Roll out dough ⅛" thick on a floured surface and fit into a 10" tart pan with a removable fluted rim.
b) Chill shell for at least 30 minutes or, covered, overnight.
c) Preheat oven to 350 degrees.

d) Line the shell with foil and fill it with rice. Bake the shell in the middle of the oven for 25 minutes.
e) Remove foil and rice carefully and Bake the shell 5 minutes more, or until pale golden. Cool shell in pan on a rack.
f) **FILLING**
g) In a blender or processor blend the filling **INGREDIENTS** until smooth. Spread blueberries evenly in the bottom of the shell.
h) Pour buttermilk filling over blueberries and bake in the middle of the oven for 30 to 35 minutes or until just set.
i) Remove the rim of the pan and cool the tart completely in the pan on the rack. Sift confectioners' sugar over the tart and serve at room temp or chilled with blueberry ice cream.

86. **Blueberry Cornmeal Cake**

Makes: 16 Makes: 2 9-inch cakes

INGREDIENTS:

Cake Batter:
- 3 cups Semolina Flour
- 1 ½ cups cornmeal
- 1 tablespoon baking powder
- 1 teaspoon salt
- 1-pound unsalted butter, softened
- 3 cups white sugar
- 8 eggs, at room temperature
- 1 ½ cups sour cream
- 1 tablespoon vanilla extract Berries:
- ½ cup unsalted butter, divided
- 1 cup brown sugar, divided
- 6 cups fresh blueberries, divided

INSTRUCTIONS:

a) Preheat the oven to 350 degrees F (175 degrees C).

b) Mix Semolina Flour, cornmeal, baking powder, and salt together in a bowl.

c) Cream together butter and sugar with an electric mixer until smooth. Beat in eggs one at a time, scraping down the bowl after each addition. Add sour cream and vanilla; combine until smooth. Add flour mixture and mix until incorporated. Set aside.

d) Divide butter between two 9-inch cast iron pans; melt over medium-low heat, about 1 minute. Add ½ of the brown sugar to each pan; cook until butter and sugar begin to bubble, 2 to 3 minutes. Divide blueberries between the two pans and remove from stove top.

e) Divide cornmeal batter between the pans; place each on a sheet pan.

f) Bake in the preheated oven until a toothpick inserted into the middle comes out clean, 45 to 50 minutes.

g) Let cool slightly, about 15 minutes. Run a knife around the outer edges of each cake and invert onto a cutting board for slicing.

87. Blueberry Boy Bait

INGREDIENTS:
- 2 cups Semolina Flour
- 1 cup sugar
- 2 teaspoons baking powder
- ¼ teaspoon salt
- ⅔ cup vegetable oil
- 1 cup milk
- 124.eggs
- 2 cups blueberries, fresh or frozen
- 2 tablespoons sugar
- 1 teaspoon cinnamon

INSTRUCTIONS:
a) Preheat oven 350 degrees and spray a 9×13-inch baking pan with nonstick cooking spray.
b) In a mixing bowl of a free standing mixer fitted with the paddle attachment mix together the flour, sugar, baking powder and salt.
c) Add the oil, milk and eggs. Mix for 3 minutes.
d) Pour batter into the prepared pan, evenly sprinkle the blueberries on top.
e) In a small bowl, combine the 3 tablespoons of sugar and cinnamon, then sprinkle over the blueberries. Bake 50 minutes or until a toothpick inserted into the center comes out clean.

88. **Mixed Berry Cobbler with Sugar Biscuits**

Makes: 10 SERVINGS

INGREDIENTS:
- Vegetable oil, for greasing
- 2 cups fresh strawberries, sliced
- 2 cups fresh blackberries
- 2 cups fresh blueberries
- 1 cup granulated sugar
- ¾ cup water
- 2 tablespoons unsalted butter
- 1 tablespoon vanilla extract
- 3 tablespoons cornstarch

FOR THE BISCUIT TOPPING:
- 2 cups Semolina Flour
- ¼ cup granulated sugar
- 3 tablespoons baking powder
- ½ teaspoon kosher salt
- ¾ cup buttermilk
- 5 tablespoons cold unsalted butter, shredded
- 2 teaspoons vanilla extract
- 2 tablespoons melted unsalted butter
- 2 tablespoons coarse sugar

INSTRUCTIONS:
a) Preheat the oven to 375 degrees F. Lightly grease a 9-by-13-inch baking dish.
b) In a large pot over medium heat, combine the berries with the sugar, water, butter, and vanilla. When bubbles start to form, scoop out about ¼ cup liquid from the pot.
c) In a small bowl, combine the ¼ cup of hot liquid with the cornstarch and mix until lump-free. Pour the cornstarch mixture back into the pot with the berries and stir. Cook until everything thickens, then pour the fruit mixture into the baking dish. Set aside.
d) For the biscuit topping, in a large bowl, combine the flour, sugar, baking powder, and salt. Whisk until well combined. Add in the buttermilk, shredded butter, and vanilla. Mix the ingredients. Scoop out the biscuit mixture and place it on top of the berry filling.
e) Brush the biscuits with melted butter, then sprinkle on the coarse sugar. Bake in the oven, uncovered, for 30 to 35 minutes. Remove from the oven, and let cool. Serve with or without ice cream.

89. Blackberry cream nut tart

Makes: 1 serving

INGREDIENTS:
- ⅓ cup Semolina flour
- ½ teaspoon Salt
- 1 8-ounce package of cream cheese, softened
- ¼ cup Sweetened condensed milk
- 2 tablespoons Sifted powdered sugar
- 1 16-ounce package of frozen blackberries, thawed and drained
- ½ cup Granulated sugar
- 3 tablespoons Cornstarch
- ½ cup Finely ground walnuts
- 1½ cups Sifted powdered sugar
- 2 tablespoons Butter-flavored shortening
- ½ teaspoon Vanilla
- ½ cup Butter-flavored shortening
- 3 tablespoons Ice water
- 1 tablespoon Fresh Yuzu juice
- ¼ cup White chocolate chips
- ¼ cup Walnuts
- 2 tablespoons Boysenberry syrup
- 1 teaspoon Butter or margarine
- ½ teaspoon Fresh Yuzu juice
- ⅛ teaspoon Salt
- ½ teaspoon Butter flavoring
- 4 tablespoons whipping cream

INSTRUCTIONS:
a)   To make the crust: Preheat oven to 425 degrees. Combine flour and salt in a bowl. Cut in shortening using a pastry blender or 2 knives until all flour is blended in to form pea-sized chunks.
b)   Sprinkle with water, 1 tablespoon at a time. Toss lightly with a fork until the dough will form a ball. Press between hands to form a 5- to 6-inch "pancake."

c) Flour the rolling surface and rolling pin lightly. Roll the dough into a circle. Trim 1 inch larger than an upside-down 9-inch tart pan with removable sizes. Loosen the dough carefully. Fold into quarters. Flour tart pan lightly.

d) Unfold the dough and press it into the tart pan. Trim the edge even with the top of the rim. Prick the bottom and sides thoroughly with a fork 50 times to prevent shrinkage.

e) Cover the edge with a double layer of foil to prevent over-browning.

f) Bake for 10 to 15 minutes or until lightly browned. Cool to room temperature.

g) To make cream cheese filling: Combine cream cheese, condensed milk, powdered sugar, and Yuzu juice in a bowl. Beat at the low speed of an electric mixer until creamy. Place white chocolate chips and nuts in a food processor work bowl. Process until finely chopped. Blend into cheese mixture. Spread in the bottom of the cooled baked tart shell.

h) To make fruit filling: Combine blackberries, sugar, cornstarch, and boysenberry syrup in a medium saucepan. Cook and stir on medium heat until the mixture is thickened and clear. Remove from heat. Stir in butter, Yuzu juice, and salt. Transfer to a bowl. Cool to room temperature. Spoon over cheese filling.

i) To make topping: Sprinkle nuts over fruit filling in a lattice fashion.

j) To garnish: Combine powdered sugar, shortening, vanilla, butter flavoring, and 3 tablespoons of cream in a bowl. Beat until smooth, adding more cream, if needed, for desired consistency. Spoon into the decorator bag fitted with the desired tip. Form a decorative border around the edge of the tart.

k) Refrigerate for 1 to 2 hours. Remove rim. Cut into servings.

l) Refrigerate leftovers.

90. Oriental semolina cake

Makes: 1 cake

INGREDIENTS:
2 pounds Wheat semolina
2½ cup Sugar
1 teaspoon Baking powder
2 cups Sour cream
2 ounces Margarine, softened
4 cups Sugar
3 cups Water or butter
¾ cup Water
3 tablespoons Tahini
½ cup Chopped pine nuts
10 Drops fresh lemon juice

INSTRUCTIONS:
a) Preheat oven to 170 C (325 F).
b) In a large bowl combine semolina, sugar, baking powder, sour cream and margarine. Gradually add water. Beat until smooth.
c) Oil a large oven pan. Spread the pan with tahini.
d) Pour the batter into the pan, sprinkle with peanuts or pine nuts, and bake 45 minutes, or until golden. Cool.
e) Make syrup: combine sugar, water and lemon juice in a large, heavy-bottomed saucepan. Cook on low heat for 20 minutes, until thick.
f) Cut the cake to 5 cm X 5 cm (2 inch X 2 inch) squares, and pour the hot syrup over the cake squares.
g) Serve immediately or at room temperature.

91. Nut-stuffed semolina pastries, cyprus style

Makes: 30 servings

INGREDIENTS:
- ¼ pounds Sweet butter
- 1¼ cup Fine semolina
- Orange flower water
- ¼ teaspoon Salt
- 3 tablespoons Warm water (more if needed)
- 1 cup Chopped unsalted pistachios
- 4½ tablespoon Granulated sugar
- 1 tablespoon Ground cinnamon
- Confectioners' sugar

INSTRUCTIONS:
a) In a small, heavy saucepan, bring the butter to bubbling over medium heat and stir in the fine semolina. Transfer to a small bowl, cover, and let stand overnight at room temperature.
b) The next day, uncover and add 2 teaspoons orange flower water, the salt, and gradually the warm water, working with your fingers to make a firm dough.
c) Knead for 5 minutes, then cover and let rest 1 hour. Meanwhile, combine the pistachios, sugar, and ground cinnamon in a small bowl.
d) Break off pieces of dough slightly larger in size than a walnut.
e) Work in your fingers to form a ball. Press the center with your thumb to make a large well and fill with 1 teaspoon of the nut mixture, then cover over with dough and shape into an oval. Set on a cookie sheet and continue until all pastries are shaped. Bake in a moderate oven (350 F) for 30 to 35 minutes or until the yellow color has become a light, not a deep, chestnut.
f) Remove to racks and cool for 10 minutes, then dip quickly into orange flower water and roll in confectioners' sugar. Cool before storing.

92. Semolina custard with a rum-raisin sauce

Makes: 1 servings

INGREDIENTS:
- 2 cups Blanched; sliced almonds
- 1 quart Water
- 1 teaspoon Almond extract
- ½ cup Agar flakes
- 1 Cup; plus 2 tablespoons
- ; maple syrup
- 1 Vanilla bean; split
- ½ teaspoon Salt
- 7 tablespoons Semolina flour
- 1½ cup Water
- 2¼ cup Apricot juice
- 2 tablespoons Rum; (optional)
- ⅔ cup Sultanas or Thompson raisins
- 1 tablespoon Arrowroot
- ½ cup Toasted; sliced almonds, for garnish

INSTRUCTIONS:
a) In a blender combine almonds and 1 quart of water. Blend until smooth.
b) Strain through two layers of damp cheesecloth and squeeze to extract 1 quart of almond milk. Pour milk into a 3 quart sauce pan. Add agar flakes, almond extract and maple syrup. Split the vanilla bean and scrape seeds into the milk. Over medium flame, bring the almond milk to a simmer and then lower the flame and whisk constantly for 2 to 3 minutes or until the agar flakes are dissolved.
c) In a second saucepan, combine the semolina flour and 1½ cups cold water.
d) Over a high flame whisk constantly until the mixture thickens. Turn off heat and add to the almond milk. Stir to combine. Pour the custard into a 2 quart pan and refrigerate until set (about 30 minutes.) While the custard sets: combine juice, rum and raisins in a saucepan to simmer for 10 minutes.
e) Make a slurry from ¼ cup cold juice and the arrowroot. Stir this into the sauce and cook for 1 to 2 minutes to until the sauce thickens. puree the custard in a food processor until creamy.
f) To serve: layer the custard, toasted almonds and raisin sauce in a wine glass and serve warm or chilled.

93. Semolina pudding

Makes: 6 servings

INGREDIENTS:
- 4½ cup milk
- 1 cup sugar
- 1 pinch salt
- 1 vanilla bean; split
- 1½ cup semolina
- 4 ounce unsalted butter
- 1 pint raspberries
- 1 cup sweetened whipped cream
- 6 sprigs mint

INSTRUCTIONS:
a) Preheat oven to 400 degrees. Bring milk, sugar, salt and vanilla bean to a boil. Using a whisk, mix in the semolina and butter. Pour into a 1½-quart baking dish. Cover and bake for 40 minutes. Garnish with the berries, cream, and mint.

94. Semolina with apples and caramel

Makes: 4 servings

INGREDIENTS:
- 125 grams Semolina
- ¾ litre Milk
- 80 grams Butter
- 300 grams Sugar
- 2 Apples

INSTRUCTIONS:
a) Peel and cut the apples in half. Remove the core and seeds with a pointed knife. Melt 40 g of the butter in a frying pan and cook the apples for 10 minutes over a low heat. When they are cooked, arrange them in a dish and put to one side.
b) Add 250 g of the sugar to the milk in a saucepan and bring to the boil, stirring continuously. Add the semolina gradually, stirring with a wooden spoon to prevent lumps forming. Add 30 g of the butter in small pieces, and cook for another 5 minutes.
c) Pour the still fairly liquid semolina over the apples and allow to cool.
d) Make a caramel sauce by melting 50 g sugar and 1 tablespoon water in a small saucepan, and cooking until the mixture darkens. Pour the caramel over the cool semolina, make a few swirls in it with a fork, and serve.

95. Sweet semolina cake with lemon syrup)

Makes: 1 8x12 flat

INGREDIENTS:
- 1½ cup Water
- 1 cup Sugar
- 12 tablespoons Butter; unsalted, melted and cooled
- 3 cups Semolina, yellow
- 3 cups Sugar
- 2 tablespoons Lemon juice, fresh
- ¼ teaspoon Rose water, bottled
- ¾ cup Cold water
- 20 Blanched almonds, whole split in half lengthwise

INSTRUCTIONS:
a) First prepare the syrup in the following fashion: combine 1« cups of water, 1 cup of sugar and the lemon juice in a small saucepan.
b) Stirring constantly, cook over moderate heat until the sugar dissolves. Increase the heat to high and cook briskly, uncovered and undisturbed, for 5 minutes (timing it from the moment the syrup boils), or until the syrup reaches a temperature of 220 degrees (F) on a candy thermometer. Remove the pan from the heat, stir in the rose water and set the syrup aside to cool.
c) Meanwhile bake the cake. Preheat the oven to 350. With a pastry brush, coat the bottom and sides of an 8 by 12 inch baking pan with 1 tablespoon of the melted butter.
d) In a deep mixing bowl, stir the semolina and 3 cups of sugar together until thoroughly combined. Stirring constantly, pour in up to ¾ cup of water, a few tablespoons at a time, using only enough to moisten all the semolina. When the mixture becomes too resistant to stir, work in the water with your hands. Then add 8 tablespoons (« cup) of the melted butter, a tablespoon at a time, and beat with a large spoon until it is absorbed.
e) Pour the batter into the baking pan, and with a metal spatula or the back of a spoon, spread it evenly into the corners of the pan.

f) then with a sharp knife and a ruler, score the surface into diamonds by making parallel lines about 2 inches apart and « inch deep, then crossing them diagonally to form diamond shapes. Gently press an almond half in the center of each diamond. Brush the cake with 3 tablespoons of melted butter and bake in the middle of the oven for 1 hour, or until the cake is firm to the touch and the top is delicately browned.

g) Remove the cake from the oven and immediately sprinkle the syrup over the top, a tablespoon or two at a time. Use only as much of the syrup as the cake will absorb readily; it should be soft but not soggy. Let the cake cool to room temperature before serving it.

96. Semolina & milk dessert

Makes: 1 Servings

INGREDIENTS:
- 125 grams Cashew nuts
- 3 Cardamoms
- 75 grams Ghee
- 12 5 g sultanas
- 250 grams Semolina
- 250 ml Milk
- 125 grams Sugar
- 3 teaspoons Rose water
- ½ teaspoon Rose essence

INSTRUCTIONS:
a) Roughly chop the cashewnuts and crush the cardamoms. Heat the ghee and fry the cashewnuts until a golden brown. Drain and remove. Fry the sultanas in the same oil, drain and remove.
b) Add the semolina to the pan and roast over a moderate heat until it is a golden brown. Heat the milk in another pan, add the sugar and when it has dissolved pour onto the semolina.
c) Cook until the liquid has been absorbed mix well and add the cashewnuts, cardamom, sultanas, rose water and rose essence. Stir well.

97. Halva (semolina candy)

Makes: 60 candies

INGREDIENTS:
- 1 cup Olive oil
- 3 cups Semolina
- 2 cups Sugar
- 3 cups Milk; combined with 1 cup water

INSTRUCTIONS:
a) In a heavy 10 to 12 inch skillet, heat the oil over moderate heat until a light haze forms above it.
b) Pour in the semolina in a slow, thin stream, stirring constantly.
c) Reduce the heat to low and, stirring occasionally, simmer for 20 minutes, or until all the oil has been absorbed and the meal turns a light golden color.
d) Add the sugar and then gradually stir in the milk and water mixture.
e) Continue cooking for about 10 minutes longer, stirring constantly until the mixture is thick enough to hold its shape almost solidly in the spoon.
f) Watch for any sign of burning and regulate the heat accordingly.
g) Pour the halva into an ungreased 6 by 10 by 2 inch baking dish, spreading it and smoothing the top with a metal spatula or the back of the spoon.
h) Cool until firm. Just before serving, cut the halva into 1 inch squares.

98. Semolina budino with berry compote

Makes: 1 servings

INGREDIENTS:
- 4 Egg yolks
- ¾ cup Sugar
- ½ teaspoon Vanilla extract
- 4 ounces Melted butter
- ¾ cup Milk
- ¼ cup Semolina flour
- ⅓ cup Cake flour
- 4 Egg whites
- 1 tablespoon Sugar
- 1 cup Berry compote;
- 1 pint Blackberries; blueberries, strawberries
- 3 tablespoons Water
- 2 tablespoons Sugar

INSTRUCTIONS:
a) Preheat oven to 325 degrees.
b) Add egg yolks and sugar to the bowl of a food processor, and using the paddle attachment beat until ribbons begin to form. At this point, add the vanilla the butter and the milk.
c) Sift the semolina and cake flour together and beat into the egg mixture.
d) In a separate bowl beat the egg white and the sugar together until medium soft peaks form.
e) Fold whites into batter and pour into sugared ramekins. Cover with aluminum foil.
f) Bake in water bath just until set. Serve slightly warm with whipped cream and berry compote.
BERRY COMPOTE:
g) In a medium saucepan over medium heat, cook the berries in the water with the sugar until they are soft. Chill and serve on top of the Budino.

99. Semolina saffron & pistachio helva

Makes: 6 Servings

INGREDIENTS:
- ½ teaspoon Saffron threads
- 2 tablespoons Hot milk
- ⅓ cup Shelled unsalted pistachios
- 9 tablespoons Unsalted butter
- 1 cup + 2 to 4 tb sugar
- 2 cups Milk
- 1 cup Semolina

INSTRUCTIONS:
a) Soak the saffron in the hot milk for at least 30 minutes. Heat a heavy frying pan and toast the pistachios with 1 tablespoon of the butter for 2 minutes, until they are lightly toasted but still green. Remove as much skin as you can from them and set aside.
b) Dissolve the sugar in the milk over low heat and keep the mixture hot. Melt the remaining butter in a heavy saucepan, add the semolina, and cook, stirring, over low heat for about 8 to 10 minutes.
c) Stir the saffron milk into the hot sugared milk and add to the semolina, and cook, stirring vigorously. Remove the helva from the fire, cover, and allow to stand in a warm spot for 15 minutes.
d) Fold in the pistachios and serve warm or at room temperature in bowls.

100. Greek Semolina Pudding

Makes: 4 servings

INGREDIENTS
- 3 cups whole milk
- 1 cup (240g) granulated sugar
- 1/4 cup (40g) fine semolina flour
- 1 tablespoon cornstarch
- 2 whole eggs
- 1 egg yolk
- 1/4 teaspoon salt
- 2 teaspoons pure vanilla extract
- 1 tablespoon butter
- optional: 1 tablespoon orange blossom water or rosewater
- Garnish:
- Chopped pistachios
- maraschino cherries

INSTRUCTIONS
a) Add the milk, salt, and half of the sugar to a saucepan. Place over medium-heat and cook until steaming hot.
b) In a mixing bowl combine the eggs, cornstarch, and remaining sugar and whisk together until smooth.
c) Temper the egg mixture by slowly adding the steaming hot milk to the egg mixture while whisking together.
d) Pour the mixture back into the saucepan and return to medium-heat. Cook will whisking constantly until it boils and thickens enough to coat the back of a spoon.
e) Remove the pan from the heat and add the butter, vanilla, and orange blossom water. Whisk together until smooth.
f) Divide the pudding into serving cups or bowls and allow to cool completely.
g) Garnish with chopped pistachios and a maraschino cherry in the center of each pudding cup.

CONCLUSION

We hope you have enjoyed this journey through the world of semolina-based dishes. Whether you are a seasoned cook or a beginner in the kitchen, we believe that you will find something to love in this cookbook. With 100 delicious recipes and plenty of tips and tricks, you'll be able to whip up a semolina-based dish for any occasion.

Semolina is a versatile ingredient that can be used in both sweet and savory dishes, making it a great addition to any pantry. From comforting bowls of creamy polenta to exotic couscous salads, there's no limit to what you can create with semolina. So why not try something new and expand your culinary horizons? We guarantee that the Semolina Cookbook will not disappoint!

Ingram Content Group UK Ltd.
Milton Keynes UK
UKHW020625050623
422885UK00009B/47

9 781835 005002